RAILWAY PHOTOGRAPHY

Brian Solomon & John Gruber

Published by

An F&W Publications Company

700 East State Street • Iola, WI 54990-0001
715-445-2214 • 888-457-2873
www.krause.com

Please, call or write us for our free catalog of publications.
Our toll-free number to place an order or obtain a free catalog is 800-258-0929
or please us our regular business telephone 715-445-2214.

ISBN: 0-87349-566-7
Library of Congress Number: 2003108891
Manufactured in China

Edited by:Tom Collins
Designed by: Davis Stanard

✳ In memory of the artist Ted Rose ✳
1940 - 2002

Photography is about philosophy and images. No two photographers will offer the same philosophy, nor will they make the same images.

There are many opinions, theories, and approaches toward railroad photography. In this book, we have sought to give the reader a variety of opinions and many perspectives from those in the field. We would like to thank everyone who participated in this project. Without their help, this book wouldn't have been possible. They have lent us their images, techniques, and advice. In this book are the works of more than 30 railway photographers complete with their credited photos.

Many of the images in this book come from our own collections. Often we travel with other photographers or other people who lend their knowledge, technique, and insight. It would be impossible to list them all.

In addition, many people have offered suggestions, discussed concepts, and pointed the way to locations, operations, literature, and to other photographers.

One of the thrills about doing this book was working with and discussing the work of the photographers we most admire. Our friend, Mel Patrick, often asks photographers who has influenced them the most. In Brian's case, the list includes his father,

Richard Jay Solomon, as well as William D. Middleton, David Plowden, Mel Patrick (Mel, you asked!), Robert A. Buck, Doug Eisele, John Gruber, and J. D. Schmid. All have work featured in this book.

In addition, Ed Nowak, Fred Jukes, Eugene Atget, Edward Steichen, numerous painters, including Turner and Whistler, and filmmakers like Buster Keaton have been influential.

Thanks to Don Gulbrandsen of Krause Publications for embracing the concept for this project. Thanks to Mike Gardner for the use of his darkroom and studio facilities. Also, thanks to Tim Doherty for proofreading and technical suggestions, to Richard Jay Solomon for loads of things including editing and the use of his extensive library. He handed Brian a Leica at age five.

Thanks to Pat Yough for tech support, Carson Burrington for ideas about the history of science and technology, and to Dennis Le Beau for the generous use of the William Bullard photo archive.

Thanks to George C. Corey for inspiration. He has been taking railroad photos for nearly 70 years and never tires of it! And last, thanks to all the railroads and railroaders who have provided fascinating subject matter over the years.

–John Gruber and Brian Solomon, March 2003

TABLE OF CONTENTS

Opposite Page: On the evening of July 21, 1991, Amtrak No. 26, the eastbound *Pioneer,* overtakes a set of helpers at Pleasant Valley, Oregon, on Union Pacific's Encina Hill. Photographers in the American West are known for their creative and subtle use of light.

Photo by Brian Solomon
Nikon F3T; 200mm f4 Nikkor; Kodachrome 25 f5.6 1/250

INTRODUCTION

✳ A wise photographer once said, "f8 and be there." You can think about photography and you can read about railways, but unless you're out there, camera in hand and ready, you won't make railway photographs. Making good photos involves combining a variety of skills at the right moment to capture what you see.

But before you can capture what you see, you must see it. What do you see when you watch the railway?

Tracks. Trains. Locomotives. People. Bridges. Tunnels. Stations. Signals. Scenery. All are elements of the railway—but don't forget motion. Railways are all about motion. Trains are big, fascinating, moving machines. They make the railway what it is. They are compelling, enthralling, and inspiring.

Isn't motion what makes us want to capture railways on film? Don't we want to preserve the thrill of watching a massive train pass? Don't we want to savor the moment, share it with others, and preserve it for posterity?

Yet motion is what makes railway photography difficult. How can you convey the power and thrill of motion in a still photo? Do you try to stop the action or work with it? Do you impart motion or ignore it? If you show motion, how can you preserve clarity?

Should you focus on the machinery and ignore what it does? Will you let the railway roll through the landscape or become the landscape? These are some of the challenges facing a railway photographer.

Detail photographs, such as this cast iron sign on the Great Western Railway at Loughborough, England, can be both informative and humorous.

Photo by Brian Solomon
Nikon F3T; 135mm f2.8 Nikkor;
Fuji Astia (RAP)

Opposite Page: At 8:25 am on October 4, 1996, Conrail TV9 (Boston to Chicago) climbs past milepost 130 near Middlefield, Massachusetts, on the old Boston & Albany. Back-lighting (primary light from behind the subject) captures the drama of moving trains.

Photo by Brian Solomon
Nikon F3T; 200mm f4.0 Nikkor;
Kodachrome 25 (KM)

Author Brian Solomon with his father Richard Jay Solomon in August 1968.

Photo by Maureen Solomon
Leica M4; 50mm f2.0 Summicron; Kodachrome II

Any photographer's success depends on the quality of the photos as much as on the subject portrayed. Subject alone cannot make a great photo. Look at your photos. Do they impart what you hoped they would? Do they capture the essence of the railway? How could you do better?

Keys to making better railway photos are your keen observation of the railroad and lighting. Look carefully before you snap. Know what you are looking at. Understand it, anticipate, and react.

Another key is to know your tools. Be comfortable with your equipment. Learn to make it work for you and be ready to use it at the right moment.

Your tools are your cameras, lenses, tripods, and film. But light is your most important tool. Light makes photography work. How you use light can define your photography. Mastering the use of

Richard Gruber took this photo at the same time and same location as the book cover photo, but on the other side of the track from his father's silhouette. John was the only one on the shadow side of the track. Dick and the other photographers had the sun to their backs.

Photo by Richard Gruber

Opposite Page: On September 26, 1991, Conrail's BUOI (Buffalo, New York, to Oak Island, New Jersey) freight rolls through the Canisteo River Valley east of Adrian, New York. Lighting and elevation are key to this composition.

Photo by Brian Solomon
Nikon F3T; 105mm f1.8; Kodachrome 25, f3.5 @ 1/250

light can be one of the most short-lived and challenging aspects of railway photography.

Unlike studio photographers, railway photographers usually don't have direct control over their light sources. While the sun rises and sets predictably, weather changes the quality of sunlight, and weather is uncertain.

The railway photographer needs to anticipate the quality of light and work with ever-changing lighting situations. Learning to use light helps you master one of your most powerful tools. Fail to work with light effectively, and you will squander your opportunity. If you make a brilliant photograph in adverse conditions, you have made the most of a difficult situation.

Remember, no photographer executes every shot perfectly, but good photographers learn from their failures. Today's missed shot could result in tomorrow's success.

On July 17, 2002, a Union Switch & Signal lower-quadrant semaphore on the former Southern Pacific Siskiyou line at Oakland, Oregon, creates a silhouette. To make a silhouette like this, expose for the bright sky and block the sun with the signal.

Photo by Tom Kline
Nikon F3; 80-200mm ED Nikkor lens;
Kodachrome 64; 1/250th @ f11

Opposite Page: On August 8, 1972, NE-1 rolls through Batavia, New York, on the Lehigh Valley mainline, parallel to New York Central's Water Level Route. Elevation, Kodachrome (ASA 25) film, and clear afternoon sun were keys to making this classic pre-Conrail image.

Photo by Doug Eisele

F-stop

An f-number is calculated by dividing the focal length by the aperture diameter. The aperture controls the amount of light entering the lens. F-numbers on lenses normally are marked to be one stop apart. Each of these doubles the amount of light as each f-'stop' gets smaller.

These stop numbers vary by the square root of two. Since $\sqrt{2}=1.414$, f1.4 allows twice as much light into the lens as f2. With each lower-numbered f-stop doubling the light, a lens may have: f22, f16, f11, f8, f5.6, f4, f2.8, f2, and f1.4.

F1.4 is eight full stops larger than f22. So f1.4 allows 256 times more light to pass (2 to the 8th power = 256). With many 35mm film format lenses, f8 is the f-stop in the middle of the range.

If you set the lens to a smaller f-number—that is, selecting a smaller aperture to let less light into the camera—you are 'stopping down.' Alternatively, if you choose a wider aperture in order to let more light into the camera, you are 'opening up.'

The intent of this book is to inspire you. We want to help you hone your observations, refine your photographic skills, master your tools, and make better railway photographs. We do this by suggestions, instructions, and examples. Ultimately how you achieve your goals is up to you.

There is no right or wrong in photographic technique, provided you are happy with your results. The tools you use, the places you photograph, and the subjects you capture are all up to you. Beware of narrow-minded dogma that demands convention, discourages creativity, or proposes to impose gratuitous structure on your photography. Rules are for the lazy—techniques are for the creative. Do what you feel works best for you and enjoy yourself.

On July 28, 1958, Richard Jay Solomon rode Chesapeake & Ohio's Train No. 6, the FFV ("Fast Flying Virginian"). A good photographer has the insight to record ordinary activities, knowing that everything will change, eventually.

Photo by Richard Jay Solomon
Kodak Retina IIIC; 35mm f4 Schneider lens; Kodachrome (ASA 10)

Opposite Page: Author John Gruber at Dresden Hbf, Germany.

Photo by Brian Solomon
Nikon N90S, 24mm f2.8 Nikkor AF lens; Fuji Sensia 100 Lens (RA)

By John Gruber
President, Center for Railroad Photography and Art

CHAPTER 1

RAILROADS & PHOTOGRAPHY

※ Railroads and photography grew up together as technologies that profoundly changed American life. It shouldn't be surprising that railroads embraced photography—and vice versa. Only a few years separate the beginnings of railroads and the perfection of photography.

Railroads sought approval from the American public and needed representations of their existence. As fast-moving subjects, railroads spurred photographers to develop ways to capture the speed of trains, the timelessness of tracks going into the sunset, and the ever-approaching Western frontier. Railroads led the way in commercial photography, and created a niche for rail-enthusiast photography.

In 1828, the Baltimore & Ohio, America's earliest commercial railroad, laid its ceremonial first stone tie at a grand July 4th celebration in Baltimore. Two years earlier, in France, Joseph Nicephore Niepce made the world's first photograph, a heliograph.

Less than a decade later, in Paris, Louis Daguerre announced the first practical photographic process. Samuel F. B. Morse, best known for his telegraph code, brought the daguerreotype to the U.S. in 1839. Undated views of locomotives *Bristol*, built in 1841 for the Western Railroad of Massachusetts, and

Tioga, built for the Philadelphia & Columbia Railroad in 1848, survive from that era.

The B&O cemented the railroad's relationship with artists and photographers by sponsoring an excursion for them in 1858. The six-car train left Baltimore's Camden Station June 1 headed for Wheeling, Virginia, on the Ohio River. One car included a darkroom for wet plate photography.

"The excursionists are a rare combination of the literary and artistic talent, and it is proposed to take photographic views, and pencil as well as pen-and-ink sketches of the most picturesque points along the road," said the *Baltimore Sun*.

Modern corporate public relations originated on the B&O as its master of transportation, William Prescott Smith (d. 1872), wrote the first corporate history in 1853, then planned four special media events—including the artists' excursion.

The Civil War offered experience of another sort as photographers learned techniques later employed in documenting western expansion and railroad building.

At least a dozen photographers recorded the progress of the transcontinental railroad's construction following the war. Arundel C. Hull (1846-1908) started out from Omaha in spring 1867,

The *Tioga* and its crew pose, probably within a year of its being built in 1848 by Norris Brothers for the Philadelphia & Columbia. The appearance of the crew and the lack of a cab provide clues to the date. Cabs didn't become common for another five years.

Copy negative from the Chaney Collection, Smithsonian Institution

The Baltimore & Ohio's four-day excursion in 1858 cemented the railroad industry's relationship with artists and photographers. The photographers and other guests are photographed near Oakland, Maryland. About 100 glass plates were exposed on the trip.

Smithsonian Institution

Arundel C. Hull is one of the hardworking photographers of the transcontinental railroad's construction. Crews helped him reach the spectacular Dale Creek bridge in Wyoming in 1868 to record the crossing of the first Union Pacific locomotive.

Eugene A. Miller Collection

traveling in Nebraska, Colorado, Wyoming, and the Utah Territories. He made and sold photographs along the Union Pacific through late fall of 1868. When he returned, Hull went to work for William Henry Jackson (1843-1942) as a portrait photographer. Jackson and Hull set out again in summer 1869 with Hull staying until December to finish their work.

Jackson, who had missed the golden spike ceremony, stayed active for more than 30 years. Although known for Colorado railroads, his work extended to both coasts and the South.

Landscape views made by Carleton E. Watkins (1828-1916), while traveling mostly in California on a railroad pass, were influenced by what he could see near the tracks.

Grand rail exhibits at the 1876 Centennial Exposition in Philadelphia and the 1893 World's Columbian Exposition in Chicago provided more photo opportunities. Frederick Gutekunst (1831-1911) was responsible for the large landscape panoramas along the Pennsylvania Railroad at the 1876 display.

In the last three decades of the 19th century, some 200 photographers toured the country in railroad photo cars, pausing in smaller communities to make portraits for the residents.

Commercial Photography

Railroads pioneered industrial photography, initially as a way to record their locomotive inventories. Builders employed photographers to document their work. For example, John Reid's studio took photos of locomotives built at Rogers, Cooke, and Grant in Paterson, New Jersey, until the last Cooke shop (then owned by American Locomotive Company) closed in 1928. Reid (1835-1911) also recorded bridges and machinery constructed in Paterson.

Railroad company-sponsored photographers promoted travel and development before other corporations had even considered the need for photography. They produced a staggering array of advertising, technical, documentary, and art photographs. Their photography also defined modern advertising.

At a time when portraits dominated the business, *Wilson's Photographic Magazine* pointed to railroads as a specialty for professional photographers. In August 1901, the editor asked readers to take a look at "... the magnificent railroad photographs which Rau, Jackson, [F. A.] Nims, and others have turned out. The work is a class by itself ..."

"Photography plays an important part in the every-day work of the modern railroad," said Edward J. Davison, a Kansas City commercial photographer. Passenger departments "... are willing to pay fair prices for desirable material, so that the field is worth cultivation."

Davison cautioned in the March 1903 *Photo-Miniature* that working for railroads is not always easy. "It is absolutely necessary to have a clear understanding of what is wanted and secure the views required as the journey is made."

To further encourage ridership, railroads established periodicals. These included *Sunset*, by Southern Pacific; *Four-Track News*, New York Central;

In 1930, Perrie Mahaffey made a night photograph of the Broadway Limited taking on water at the track pans at Latrobe, Pennsylvania. He spread flash powder for 500 feet along the right of way.

California State Railroad Museum

Opposite Page: Manufacturers produced extremely high quality photographs of their new locomotives. These images were exposed on large format plates that could be used to make contact prints. The background was opaqued in negative to appear white in the final image.

Lima Locomotive Works photo

John Reid recorded an Erie Railway train opening the Rosendale Bridge in the Wallkill Valley of New York. The print is from an original glass plate in the Munson Paddock Collection at the Donnelly Library, Lake Forest College, Lake Forest, Illinois.

Paddock Collection at the Donnelly Library, Lake Forest College in Illinois

William Bullard was a Worcester, Massachusetts-based professional photographer, who pioneered railroad action photographs. This 1900 photograph of an east-bound Boston & Albany freight was made using a view camera and exposed on a Stanley Dry Plate.

Photo by William Bullard, courtesy of Dennis Le Beau

Book of the Royal Blue, B&O; *Black Diamond Monthly*, Lehigh Valley; *Maine Central*; and *Frisco System*.

Photographing fast-moving trains in the late 1890s and early 1900s required ingenuity and technical knowledge. Frank W. Blauvelt (1850-1929) in the New York area, William Bullard (1877-1918) in Worcester, Massachusetts, J. Foster Adams (1882-1962) in Wisconsin, and M. Fred Jukes (1877-1971) in Wyoming and Nevada, were among the earliest practitioners of action photography.

An illustration of the close association between railroads and photography was the 1900 promotional effort of the Chicago & Alton, which hired George R. Lawrence (1867-1938) of Chicago to build the world's largest camera for a photo of the Alton Limited.

High quality halftone reproduction of photographs on the printed page, developed in the early 1900s, further expanded the use of camera work. Photography was so vital that when the Southern Pacific lost its files in the San Francisco earthquake and fire of 1906, it immediately sent photographers in two photo cars to replace the images.

Each railroad took a different approach to pho-

William Henry Jackson toured the Chicago & North Western line in 1898 and stopped at Devil's Lake, Wisconsin. The Photochrom print was made by a Swiss process used by Detroit Publishing Company that turned black and white negatives into color views.

Colorado Historical Society

Early action photographer M. Fred Jukes often made photographs along the Union Pacific. The UP photo here is near Rawlings, Wyoming, where Jukes operated a studio. *Railway & Locomotive Engineering* encouraged its readers to submit action photos. It published the photo in 1904.

California State Railroad Museum

tographic services. The Pennsylvania tended to rely on photographers spread across its system, while the Southern Pacific built up a central bureau in its San Francisco headquarters, with a satellite facility in Los Angeles.

Mileage reached a peak in 1916, with 254,037 miles of line in service, then started on a long decline, yet photographic activities remained strong for another 40 years.

In 1921, King D. Ganaway won the first prize in the 15th annual Wanamaker's Department Store photographic exhibition in Philadelphia with "Spirit of Transportation." It showed two sections of the Twentieth Century Limited in Chicago.

Pictorial photography, often with leadership from skilled amateurs, encouraged popular activities such as camera clubs and exhibitions. It brought new energy to industrial and advertising photogra-

phy in the 1920s. William M. Rittase (1887-1968) wrote in *Photo-Era* magazine how locomotives in the railroad yard "are overpowering, energetic, and filled with romance."

Three close-ups, made for the Reading Railroad, accompanied a *New York Times* review of the *Men and Machines Exhibit* of 1930. The reviewer quoted Margaret Bourke-White (1904-1971) as saying that "… any important art coming out of the industrial age will draw inspiration from industry, because industry is alive and vital."

Fortune magazine gave Bourke-White, Rittase, and others a larger and more influential audience. Beginning in 1936, *Life* built increasing interest in photography and photo stories.

Railroads enthusiastically adopted new types of photography. The Union Pacific pioneered outdoor color photography in 1929, replacing paintings in

its advertising.

Photographers shot hundreds of thousands of railroad photos in the 20th century. John W. Barriger III, who got his first railroad job in 1917, amassed some 50,000 photographs—many of them taken while he was chief of the Railroad Division of the Reconstruction Finance Corporation from 1934 through 1941. His work shows the influence of railroad corridors in the American landscape.

As the nation's rail center, Chicago attracted commercial railroad photographers. Kaufmann & Fabry had more than a dozen railroad clients. Hedrich-Blessing, a leader in architectural and industrial photography founded in 1928, served at least three large railroads. In 1956, the Chicago

King D. Ganaway's "Spirit of Transportation" shows the 20th Century Limited in Chicago in 1918. An African-American butler, he learned photography on his days off. In 1921, this photo captured first prize in the 15th annual Wanamaker's Department Store exhibition in Philadelphia.

From Fort Dearborn Magazine, *a journal that published many of Ganaway's photos*

Philadelphia studio pictorial photographer William Rittase worked for Eastern railroads in the 1930s and 1940s. His Reading photo shows locomotive 2102 as it was rebuilt 1945. The spectacular cloud came from a second negative, double-printed in the darkroom.

Far Left: Railroad people long have been the subject of photographers. This 1905-1910 view of a railroad mechanic at Worcester, Massachusetts, was made with a view camera on a 4 x 5 Stanley Dry Plate. The man is repairing a freight car with a broken knuckle.

Photo by William Bullard, courtesy of Dennis Le Beau

Burlington & Quincy sandwiched two of its negatives to show its new Denver *Zephyr* on the suburban line near Chicago with Glacier National Park's mountains in the background.

A Chicago publication inaugurated in 1944, *Negro Traveler*, made an unusual use of publicity photos. Editors Clarence E. Markham (1911-1995) and his wife, Olga, published photos "… to create a greater sense of pride …" among African Americans working on the trains.

Photographing new equipment properly was critical for promotional efforts. Operating departments permitted photographers to stop fast passenger trains for a few minutes, sometimes with unfortunate results. When Santa Fe system photographer R.

Collins Bradley (1917-2002) stopped the San Francisco *Chief* in California, the train took off without a brakeman who had been protecting the rear of the train.

Company photography departments reached a peak in this post-World War II streamliner era. Among other names are Nicholas Morant of the Canadian Pacific; the Erie's John Long; Ed Nowak of the New York Central; and Steve Edwards of the Southern Pacific. With the 1971 transfer of passenger services to Amtrak, most company photographic departments were abolished. The New York City area commuter railroads are an exception.

Photographers played an important role in projecting a positive image of the railroad. Santa Fe system photographer R. Collins Bradley caught a freight train in Crozier Canyon, 30 miles east of Kingman, Arizona, about 1959.

John Gruber Collection

To publicize its fast merchandise trains, Illinois Central lined up five locomotives in Chicago at night. The photo was the cover of IC's magazine in 1937. Arthur Adolph Presler made the photo for Kaufmann & Fabry, a Chicago commercial studio.

The Horn Collection

This Lewis Hine photograph of a Pennsylvania Railroad engineer with locomotive 3148 won an award from the New York Art Directors Club. Hine, known for his photographs of child labor, introduced his series of work portraits in 1921 with the PRR photos.

Photo by Lewis Hine from Survey, *Graphic edition*

Representations of Work

It's appropriate that Lewis Hine introduced his work portraits in 1921 with images of railroaders, since at that time the railroad industry was the largest single non-farm employer in the U.S.

Hine (1874-1940), known earlier for his photos of child labor, made the portraits on the Pennsylvania Railroad. The Pennsylvania, in turn, published the photos in its dining car menus and won an award for Hine from the New York Art Directors Club for the view of engineer Edward Reynolds (1859-1934), Rahway, New Jersey. Reynolds served the PRR for 48 years.

Less known is his work for the Erie, which published some 16 of his portraits of Erie railroaders in its magazine in 1924-'25. Hine continued with at least 80 railroad negatives through "A Railroad Fireman" in *Fortune* in 1939.

Examples from other photographers are scattered. Sol Libsohn's "Diesel Power Story" for the Standard Oil photographic library in 1947 is more about people than oil. Illinois Central showed an "able railroader—and good citizen" in its newspaper ads for June 1948. David Plowden did a project for the Smithsonian for the 1976 bicentennial celebration. The *Texas Monthly* published "Workin' on the Railroad: A Forgotten Profession" in 1992. From *Trains,* there are Ted Benson's "On-Time Tyner and the

Valley Boys" in 1983, and my Green Bay and Western story in 1994.

Three books stand out: Simpson Kalisher's *Railroad Men,* 1961; Stuart Leuthner's *The Railroaders,* in 1983; and Lina Bertucci's depiction of Milwaukee Road workers in *Railroad Voices* in 1998. Bertucci and her aunt, Cindy Angelos, were the first women brakemen hired by the Milwaukee Road in 1974. Bertucci carried her camera on the job while studying photography at the University of Wisconsin-Milwaukee.

Although thousands of employee portraits (crews with engines, cabooses, and buildings, or shop staff lined up for official views) made before about 1930 tell a part of the story, the work itself is under-represented in the visual world. To fill this gap, the Center for Railroad Photography and Art has started a three-year program, "Representations of Railroad Work, Past and Present," with funds from the North American Railway Foundation. It is an educational exhibit and publishing program to interpret railroad labor and work history using photographs and individual case histories. The project offers the opportunity to focus attention on people—one of those missing links in the photographic record of railroads.

Enthusiast Photography

Although three amateurs traveled on the B&O's excursion in 1858, amateur photography didn't become widespread until George Eastman announced the Kodak camera in 1888, daylight loading film in 1891, and a pocket Kodak in 1895.

Many photographers, such as Charles B. Chaney (1875-1848) specialized in locomotive views. In 1911, William G. Landon (1892-1979) showed a pioneering panned view of the New Haven's *Bay State Limited.* Fred Eidenbenz (1894-1970) was known for his work in the 1920s. Alfred W. Johnson (1896-1972) brought a graphic artist's eye to his photography.

Railroad Man's Magazine, 1906 to 1919, revived in 1929, evolved into today's *Railfan & Railroad.* In the 1930s, the International Engine Picture Club

Lucius Beebe carefully selects images for his books at the Pullman Company's offices on the south side of Chicago. Melvin Horn, Pullman's photographer, often recorded the visits from Beebe and his partner, Charles Clegg. Beebe's flamboyant style captivated readers.

The Horn Collection

directed its members into roster photography.

Beginning in 1938, books by Lucius Beebe (1902-1966) focused national attention on railroad photography. Beebe prepared an article about photography for the first issue of *Trains*. In a 1948 edition of *Mixed Train Daily*, Charles M. Clegg (1916-1979) set the standard for judging other photographs of traditional railroading.

Trains, founded in 1940, soon became an outlet for creative photography and encouraged innovative rail photographers. David P. Morgan (1927-1990), editor from 1953 to 1987, promoted legendary names like Philip Hastings (1925-1987), James Gallagher (1920-2002), Robert Hale (1912-1992), James Shaughnessy, Richard Steinheimer, Don Wood, and others. Kalmbach Publishing Company reprinted Morgan's 1950s farewell to steam travels with Hastings as *The Mohawk that Refused to Abdicate* in 1975.

Each decade brought new faces, such as John Gruber and Mel Patrick in the 1960s, Ted Benson in the 1970s, Blair Kooistra in the 1980s, and Joel Jensen and Gary Benson (1955-1997) in the 1990s.

Steam-era photographers were diverse. The New England Group included Shaughnessy, Hastings, Albert Hale, Thomas J. McNamara, Kent Cochrane, H. W. Pontin, William S. Young, George C. Corey, and Stanwood K. Bolton Jr. The Mid-Atlantic Group included Bob Collins, Robert Malinoski, Wood, Gordon Roth, John Briggs, John Krause, and J. J. Young. The Mid-Atlantic and Southern was composed of Herbert Harwood, Gallagher, Don Philips, H. Reid, and J. Parker Lamb.

The Midwest Group included Gruber, Mike Schafer, and William D. Middleton. Dick Kindig and Otto Perry worked in the Colorado region. Hale, Steinheimer, Stan Kistler, Gordon Glattenburg, John Illman, Benson, and Donald Duke worked in California. The Pacific Northwest included Ronald Nixon and Warren McGee.

By the 1960s, when steam was gone in the

U.S., many steam-era photographers became world travelers. The 21st century search for steam continues in such locations as Poland and China.

Magazines have provided many more outlets, but their numbers declined. *Passenger Train Journal*, founded in 1968 by Kevin McKinney, provided a venue for passenger train photography. Under the editorial direction of Kevin Keefe, and from 1983-'90 by Mike Schafer, and Carl Swanson, it pushed published passenger train photography to new limits.

In 1986, Mark Smith launched *Locomotive & Railway Preservation*. *Vintage Rails* magazine began in 1995 and offered another broadly based view of the rail scene. Pentrex discontinued publications in 1996 and 1999. Mark Hemphill, named *Trains* editor in 2000, pro-

In 1911, William G. Landon showed a scenic view of the New York Central *Limited* along the Hudson River. Landon also is known for pioneering panned photos of such trains as the *20th Century Limited* and New Haven's *Bay State Limited*.

California State Railroad Museum

Not all railroad photos need a train to be successful as James P. Gallagher's view of the Baltimore & Ohio's old main line at Relay, Maryland, illustrates. Gallagher produced remarkable black and white photographs of the 1950s steam-to-diesel transition.

Center for Railroad Photography and Art Collection

Far Right: On St. Patrick's Day 1957, Jim Shaughnessy caught a westward Nickel Plate Road freight, led by Lima-built Berkshire 772, at North East, Pennsylvania. Shaughnessy's railway photos often work in a human element giving the railroad life.

Photo by Jim Shaughnessy

Opposite Page: David Plowden praises Jim Shaughnessy's view of Boston & Maine 3713 on its last run on April 22, 1956. "Your photograph of the farewell run of that grand old B&M P-4 is my all time favorite steam engine picture. You got it all," Plowden wrote to Shaughnessy.

Photo by Jim Shaughnessy

vides an outlet for creative new photographic styles.

The Internet also has transformed the way photographers get information. The Internet now allows free exchange of information about trains.

Until the 1940s, most photographs were in black and white. With the use of Kodachrome film (beginning in 1936) and slide mounts (which were introduced in 1939) and multi-color printing presses, color took on a greater role and eventually dominated.

From the 1960s on, enthusiast photography has embraced a variety of focal length lenses. Among the first published enthusiast photos using telephoto lenses was the "remarkable movie-like sequence" of train 58 at Tunnel City, Wisconsin, in the 1961 *Trains* magazine.

The 1994 introduction of Fuji Provia film improved opportunities for spectacular night-time, natural-light time exposures. Electronics and digital cameras are bringing another revolution in photography.

Ted Benson's *One Track Mind* (2000) launched the Boston Mills masters of railroad photography series. It was edited by Greg McDonnell, an accomplished photographer. The second volume, *Steel Wheels Rolling* (2001), featured J. Parker Lamb.

Beginning in 1969, large-screen slide shows, with background sound, provided another outlet. Inspired by a photo story in the August 1965 *Trains*, Mel Patrick prepared "Chicago Union Station—A Photographic Narrative." Photos were selected to produce a coherent match between sight and sound. The concept of using narration and music to accompany slides didn't originate with Patrick, but his was the first full-scale attempt at a railroad theme program.

The idea spread across the country, and WinterRail, the largest, presented its 25th anniversary show in California in March 2003.

Recognition of the importance and artistic merit of railroad photography has steadily increased. The Railway & Locomotive Historical Society began conferring achievement awards to photographers in 1982, and established a photo award in 1984. Ted Benson added to the long list of accomplishments of Steinheimer, a 1983 R&LHS award winner. He called Steinheimer the "Ansel Adams of railroading" in *Vintage Rails* and the 1999 book *Done Honest and True*. W. W. Norton's book, scheduled to be published in fall 2004, places Steinheimer's work in a fine-art context.

The Center for Railroad Photography and Art, founded in 1997, is committed to presenting and interpreting provocative, visually exciting images of railroading. It brings together history, history of technology, visual culture studies, and geography.

Mainstream publishers have given railroad photography a wider audience. For David Plowden, a boyhood love of steam locomotives got him started in photography. "As a child, I adored the steam

Canadian Pacific train M160 about to leave Chipman for Norton, New Brunswick, on August 9, 1956. The 4-4-0 locomotive was built by Canadian Pacific in 1887. Photographer George C. Corey says, "… an operating 4-4-0 in regular service was a novelty."

Photo by George C. Corey

engine. I aspired to be a locomotive engineer." His first published photograph appeared in a 1954 *Trains*, a year before he graduated from Yale University. He worked as an assistant to the trainmaster for the Great Northern for about a year in Minnesota.

An Easterner most of his life, Plowden has lived in Winnetka, Illinois, since 1978. Plowden's record includes 20 books. In 2002, a full revision of *Bridges the Spans of North America* was published.

He says he has spent most of his career one step ahead of the wrecking ball. After photographing railroads early in the 1960s, he turned his camera to disappearing American icons like steamboats,

stations, bridges, and barns.

O. Winston Link (1914-2001) is known for his Norfolk & Western night views. They were made from 1955 to 1960 during the last days of steam. He sold his first N&W photos to New York's Museum of Modern Art in about 1976 and had his first American and European museum exhibitions in 1983. Link's work was special on two counts.

The first was his lighting. He made action shots by night with huge arrays of synchronized flashbulbs. Second, his work documented community life along the steam railroad line.

Starlight on the Rails (Abrams, 2000), an 18-year effort of Jeff Brouws and Ed Delvers, showed night railroad photographs by 23 photographers. Movement and time exposure were key factors in the photo selection. Initially, Brouws and Delvers had difficulty finding a publisher. Changes in individual photographic styles and a willingness by mainstream rail publishers to print more experimental photography helped make the book possible.

A Preservation Discipline

Railroad photography transcended its origins as a creative hobby or tool of railroad promotion. It emerged as a legitimate preservation discipline. Its images are widely recognized as a distinct form of visual art and a powerful research tool.

Beginning with a formal, 1978 exhibition at the Baltimore Museum of Art, a succession of popular and museum exhibitions have brought the work of railroad photographers and artists before millions of people.

By far the most visible exhibition was the 2002 Los Angeles exhibit at the J. Paul Getty Museum called "Railroad Vision," with 90 images from the Americas, Europe, and South Africa.

In the Getty's illustrated brochure, assistant curator Anne M. Lyden, who was in charge of the exhibition, wrote:

"From the 1850s onward photography and

Trains editor David P. Morgan introduced a "remarkable movie-like sequence" of eight telephoto lens photos to readers in 1961. They were made with a 180mm lens on a Pentax 35mm camera with a hand-operated rapid advance lever. Two of the photos are reproduced here.

Photos by John Gruber

the railroad embarked on a journey together. This complex new relationship shaped a visual culture that dealt with issues of space, time, and distance in a way that never before existed."

Also in 2002, "Traveling the Pennsylvania Railroad: The Photographs of William H. Rau" was at the Library Company of Philadelphia. The University of Pennsylvania Press, in cooperation with the Library Company, published a companion volume, edited by John C. Van Horne with Eileen E. Drelick.

A museum honoring Link's photography is opening in the former passenger station in Roanoke.

The Center's exhibit, "Railroads and Photography: 150 Years of Great Images," has been touring the country since 1999. The Center's Web site (www.railphoto-art.org) includes its list of the 20 most memorable rail photographs of the 20th century.

Archival collections held by nonprofit institutions continue to grow in quality and quantity. Railroad images are continuing to become more accessible and available to the public eye. Some 20 major depositories have an estimated 2.6 million images, according to a survey by the Center. Images at seven of these locations are available on the World Wide Web.

Railroad photography often has been overlooked as an artistic discipline. But after 160 years in a pivotal role in the industry's life and evolution, the rest of the world is "discovering" the power of railroad images.

Railroading provided Americans with the tool they needed to settle the continent and create an entirely new way of life. Photography made it possible for virtually everyone to enjoy unprecedented access to an incredible selection of images. And it changed the way we perceived our world.

Railroad photographs are much more than train pictures. As works of creative art, they bring us closer to understanding our shared heritage. They continue to fascinate us long after their moment in time.

David Plowden

"Forget yourself, think about the subject," says David Plowden, who has been responsible for 20 books about America throughout his 45-year photographic career.

"Let the subject speak for itself, don't get in its way."

Whether teaching a semester-long college course or a weekend workshop, Plowden starts with the same set of instructions. Go without a camera. Walk around the block. Look at the landscape. Become familiar with light and texture. He wants his students to "see." David says photography only can begin after this "filmless" introduction.

"It was always my sense to go out and get things like they were. I have taken blades of grass down or cut a twig that was in the way, but I have never moved anything around. I always use natural light, because that is what I see when I look at a subject. Artificial light would change everything," he continues.

A boyhood love of steam locomotives got him started in photography.

"As a child, I adored the steam engine. That was the most exciting thing in the world."

He has had more than 35 one-person exhibitions, a host of magazine articles, and a Guggenheim fellowship.

"One of the things in railroad photography today that I find disturbing is the over use of the telephoto lens. I also think it is a very hard thing to photograph diesel engines ad infinitum. There are many other interesting things to photograph including the people who work on the railroad, bridges, buildings, and yards."

"I am not a color photographer. I haven't done color in years and years," Plowden explains about his preference for black and white photography.

"I learned very quickly from my students who are color photographers that color has a language of itself, an architecture. The color of light becomes a crucial factor in color photography. There is a profound difference between black and white and color—as great a difference as there is between film and still."

David Plowden found H. R. Birkhead in Frederick, Oklahoma, on a Friday evening in July 1968. The 80-year-old agent was retiring after working for 60 years for the Missouri-Kansas-Texas Railroad. Soon after he photographed Birkhead sitting at the edge of his desk, Birkhead took the key to the depot door off his ring and dropped it in the mailbox. "… for the new man on Monday morning," he said. No one else was there to wish him well. Plowden's print, sent several months later, was returned "addressee unknown."

Traditionally, David has done all his own darkroom work. He has decided to learn more about computers and their continued influence on photography.

At age 70, David has several other photographic books in the works, and has no intention of retiring. He continues teaching at Grand Valley State University in Allendale, Michigan.

He tells students to take a look around their hometown and to begin making a record of what they see, before it changes and disappears.

CHAPTER 2

CHOOSING A CAMERA SYSTEM

✳ The tools you'll use for making railroad photographs are cameras, lenses, and other photographic apparatus. Your camera system can define the quality of images you make. Select a camera system that will allow you to make the most of your photography.

Camera systems vary widely in format, flexibility, quality, and cost. Choosing the most appropriate is a project. There is no single camera system that is best for every person or application. While high quality cameras tend to have higher prices, cost alone doesn't necessarily equate with quality.

Just because a photographer spends a lot of money on the latest, most expensive equipment, doesn't necessarily mean he or she is buying the best camera for the job, nor does it imply the photographer will get better results.

If a short line railroad spends $3 million on the latest high horsepower traction diesel-electric, will they be better able to switch their cars? No. In fact, they're much better off with a second-hand GP38 that will perform much better for their application. The same is true with camera selection.

If you spend $20,000 on a brand new 8x10" Sinar studio view camera, will you have the flexibility and the versatility you desire to make railway photos? Probably not. A less expensive system will likely give you more appropriate tools.

Format

If you visit a large professional camera store or camera show, or browse through the pages of a professional camera catalog, you will find dozens of cameras in a variety of different formats. There are numerous brands, most incompatible with one another. New models are being developed all the time. Choosing the right camera for railroad photography can be a daunting task. We will focus on film cameras, leaving the discussion of digital cameras for another chapter.

Traditionally, the camera format has been described by the size of film used. The most common camera formats used today are 35mm, 120mm "medium format," and various "large format" sizes—from 4 x 5 " to 8 x 10 " . Within each of these size categories are a variety of camera types and models. Specialized formats, such as panoramic and underwater cameras, are made for various film sizes. In addition, there are formats that are marketed largely toward snapshot photographers.

35mm Rangefinder Cameras

The 35mm is the most common format used by railway photographers. There are several basic types of 35mm cameras sold today. Many simple, automatic

◀

At sunrise on March 14, 2002, a westbound BNSF intermodal train is at Tehachapi, California. The 35mm SLR with a fast zoom lens is preferred by many top photographers. Adjusting focal length to fit the situation can offer you just the right shot.

Photo by Howard Ande
Nikon F5; 80-200 f2.8 Nikkor zoom lens; Fuji Velvia

rangefinder cameras are aimed at the amateur market. Amateur "point and shoot" cameras are the most common and are fine for family photos and even some casual railway photos. For the most part, they are too limiting for use in detailed railway photography and are not recommended for most serious work.

"Point and shoot" cameras are relatively low cost, compact, light weight, and simple. High quality "point and shoot" cameras are made, but they tend to be expensive. Their disadvantages include inflexibility and the inability to manually select aperture and shutter speeds. The majority of "point and shoots" are equipped with a simple zoom lens and small apertures. They use simple autofocus systems that cause a slight delay from the time the shutter button is pressed until the shutter actually opens.

Unlike the simple automatic snapshot cameras, a variety of high-quality 35mm rangefinder cameras provide both flexibility and precision. Several exemplary rangefinders are available, including those from Leica, Contax, and Voigtländer Bessa.

The best rangefinders feature sharp, interchangeable lenses. A rangefinder doesn't use a mirror and prism. This allows compact cameras with smaller lenses.

Rangefinders require few moving parts, so are less prone to failure and produce less camera vibration. Lower camera vibration allows for sharper images, and also allows a camera to be handheld at slower shutter speeds. Rangefinders are quieter than SLRs, and are more reliable. They are good tools for working with wide-angle and normal lens formats, and can be used effectively for making pan images.

Disadvantages are difficulties making sharp photos with telephoto lenses. The inability to see through the lens makes telephoto composition abstract, and can make precise focusing challenging. Also, the viewfinder of a rangefinder camera generally offers a smaller field of view than a good SLR. That makes composing images more challenging. Close-up and detail photos may best be made with another camera.

Rangefinders tend to be among the most expensive 35mm systems. This is partly a result of

the high quality optics used, and the precision quality of rangefinder bodies.

Several rangefinder brands, such as Leica, have become collectors' items, which is unfortunate for camera users because it drives up their price without adding quality.

35mm Single Lens Reflex Cameras

Since the mid-1960s, the 35mm SLR has been a dominant camera type used by journalists, amateurs, and railway photographers. The 35mm SLR is the preferred tool of many railway photographers. It's versatile, flexible, relatively easy to use, easy to load, readily available, and is affordable. Its compact size offers advantages over larger formats. 35mm negatives are large enough for most purposes and are ideal for publication.

For cost, convenience, and ease of use, a good 35mm SLR is hard to beat. The ability to see through the lens, using a mirror and prism, keeps the view in normal perspective. It is a great tool for composing images, especially when using telephoto and wide-angle lenses, as well as filters. If you are making close-up images, or working with very long

Three photos were made on the New York City IRT Division Flushing Line with different camera systems.

The far left photo was made with a Nikon N90S and manual focus 180mm lens. Exposure was calculated using the camera meter in 'matrix' mode, with Fuji Sensia 100 (RA) film.

A Canon EOS-3 with an auto-focus 70-200mm zoom was used to make the center photo on Ektachrome E100G film. Exposure was calculated by the in-camera metering system.

The photo above was made with a Contax G2 rangefinder and a 28mm autofocus Biogon lens. Exposure was calculated manually. The film was Fuji Sensia 100 (RA).

Far left and center photos by Brian Solomon
Above photo by Patrick Yough

telephoto lenses, your ability to see through the lens is a compositional must.

SLR system motor drives are especially useful for photos of moving trains. Several companies produce a range of 35mm SLRs—from amateur to rugged professional models. It's easy to be bamboozled by the array of products. Shop carefully before you buy so you get the flexible camera you need to make great train photographs.

Many cameras come with autofocus, auto exposure, and a variety of modes. Make sure you can easily disengage these features and operate the camera manually. A strictly automatic SLR can be too limiting and that makes the camera just a step better than a snapshot camera. Your camera should have manual exposure and focus settings.

Modern cameras offer shutter speeds at least as fast as 1/1000th of a second. This is sufficiently fast to stop most railway action. If you plan to make night photographs, slower shutter speeds are necessary. Be sure to check the camera's *slowest* speed.

Also invaluable for night work are provisions for a 'B' setting (it holds the shutter open indefinitely,

provided the shutter button is held down) or a 'T' setting (it allows the shutter to stay open indefinitely without holding the shutter button). A tripod and cable release are recommended for these settings.

Make sure the camera can accept a cable release. Some modern cameras only accept specialized electronic cable releases, which give you a variety of time-exposure options, but you'll need to buy a more expensive cable release. The traditional mechanical cable release is less expensive and may be preferable for night work.

Check to see if you can make double exposures. In normal situations it isn't desirable, but the ability to make double exposures can be useful for night photography. A depth-of-field preview option is another nice feature and allows you to temporarily close the lens aperture to see the effect of smaller f-stops. It can be used to determine your best focus point, especially with a telephoto lens.

Does the camera body come with a motor drive? How quickly does it work? A motor winder usually will give you one to two frames per second—not fast enough for most railway action. If you intend to make multiple images of trains in action, a motor drive that works at four to six frames per second will be more appropriate.

Taking multiple images is useful because it gives you extras for publication purposes. It's cheaper to take an extra slide than to duplicate one—and a dupe cannot equal the quality of an original slide.

Some camera bodies, like the traditional, mechanical Nikon FM-2, don't have built-in drives. Separate drives are available. A manual rewind can be advantageous if you want to change film in the middle of a roll. Often, modern cameras use an automatic rewind that activates when the film reaches the end of the roll.

One of the most important qualifications of any camera is how it feels in your hand. Is the camera well-balanced and easy to hold? Does it feel right? Is

On Oct. 3, 1964, Richard Jay Solomon used two Leica rangefinders—an M2 loaded with Kodachrome II (ASA 25), with a meter and a 50mm Leitz f/2 Dual-Range Summicron lens, and an M3 loaded with a high-speed Ektachrome with a 135mm Leitz f/4 Elmar lens. He also has a medium-format Rolleiflex Model T with an f3.5 Zeiss Tessar lens, loaded with Kodak Plus-X film.

Photo by Alan Schreibman

Top, Right: Today's fast films make great low-light photos possible. Don't overlook capturing the railroad in crummy weather. On Jan. 25, 1990, a westward Soo Line freight hits snow at a Brookfield, Wisconsin, grade crossing on the old Milwaukee Road.

Photo by Mike Danneman
Pentax ME Super; SMC Pentax-A f4 200mm lens; Kodachrome 200 1/500

the viewfinder bright enough? Does it appear sharp when you look through it? If you wear glasses, can you see clearly through it? Does the camera make you want to take photographs? A camera that seems awkward and intimidating may not be right for you.

What is the camera body made from? Durability is important if you're investing in a camera you hope to use for many years. A traditional metal body, such as those used by Nikon's F3, is durable, but may be heavier than modern composite material cameras.

Make sure the model has a good repair record. A shoddily made camera or one with a reputation for failure isn't what you want to bring on a long railway photo trip. Camera failure is frustrating and disappointing.

One feature sometimes incorporated in high-end SLR models is a removable prism. It's useful if you want to shoot from the hip or make very low

angle photographs. The side-mounted alternative shutter release is useful, especially for vertical images.

When you compare different 35mm cameras, consider what each system offers in the way of lenses. Generally, each manufacturer uses its own lens coupling system. Select a camera system you can expand on and one that offers a full range of lenses. Otherwise, you may be faced with changing systems as your photography matures.

A good camera system will allow interchangeability among various lenses and cameras. Starting with a relatively inexpensive body and gradually working your way up will allow you to continue using the same type of lens mount. Be sure professional lenses will couple with your body, even if you cannot afford them right away.

One of the most debatable questions in photography is which camera system is best. Almost every photographer you meet will have firm

Burlington Northern Santa Fe's Z-MEMRIC-1-07 (Memphis, Tennessee to Richmond, California) negotiates the S-curves at Caliente, California, at 5:43 p.m. on Sept. 9, 2000. Good equipment and your comfort using it facilitates high-quality railway photography.

Photo by Dave Burton
Minolta X700; 85mm lens;
Fuji Provia 100F (RDPIII) exposed @ f6.5 1/500

Photographer Brian Jennison works in the California Tehachapis on March 29, 1992, with two generations of Nikon SLRs. On the Gitzo tripod with dual ball heads are a pair of F2s. The camera on the left is fitted with a 200mm f4 Nikkor lens and the camera on the right with a 105mm f2.5 Nikkor lens. Around his neck is an F3HP with a 35mm Nikkor lens. All three cameras were loaded with Brian's choice film: Kodachrome 25.

Photo by Brian Solomon
Nikon F3T, 105mm f1.8 Nikkor lens;
Kodachrome 25

The Ultimate "Grab" Shot   by Ben Crouch

When it's 35-degrees-below-zero, your thoughts don't naturally gravitate toward just getting that great shot. Rather, they tend toward survival. That cold was what greeted us on the morning of January 28, 1958, as we exited the Plymouth Hotel in Fort Fairfield, Maine.

If survival was an overstatement, certainly keeping the Ford's heater at full blast wasn't! We headed east across the border to the Canadian Pacific Railway's delightful, historic terminal at Aroostook Junction, New Brunswick. Local intelligence had revealed the gelid conditions wouldn't preclude a late morning departure of *No. 85*, the third class freight for Presque Isle, Maine, on CPR's *Aroostook Sub.*

We spent several hours savoring the atmosphere around the yard and engine house. Finally D-10h 990, a classic CPR 4-6-0, moved off the turntable, coupled to its train and, after the usual interruptions, headed out of town. By then, the temperature had moderated, but storm clouds were showing on the western horizon, an omen of the blizzard that would set in during the late afternoon.

After crossing back into the States, we pushed ahead of *No. 85* as it worked the potato sheds in Fort Fairfield. The Route 1A road crossing at Goodwin looked to be a good spot for a run by, especially as the clouds were persistently moving closer and the bright morning sun was in jeopardy. *No. 85* finally appeared just ahead of the front edge of the storm clouds, the shot was had and we pressed on.

I must digress to highlight the mechanics of the 4x5 Speed Graphic, my camera of choice at the time. I can only compare the camera's operation as the equivalent of a present generation driver dealing with Henry Ford's challenging Model T with its hand-crank starting, planetary transmission and lack of power steering or hydraulic braking.

The Speed Graphic, while taking fantastic photos with a 4x5 negative image, was a royal pain in the butt. Two shutters—one conventional and one focal plane, focused by a knurled knob—moved the lens back or forward on a horizontal track. A 16-exposure film pack enclosed in a holder required

Photo by H. Bentley Crouch

pulling a tab to ready the next frame for exposure. A slide had to be removed from the holder before each exposure and placed back before rewinding the focal plane shutter. (Think double exposure.) And no light meter.

Needless to say, chasing trains in a narrow time frame was a challenge. Which brings us back to *No. 85.*

That narrow time frame was immediately upon us, as only about a mile west of Goodwin was a settlement known as East Lyndon. We had never been there before, and, the revelation of a possible broadside shot was suddenly and unexpectedly thrust at us. No. 85 was making good time and was closing fast. That meant this shot involved slamming on the brakes, grabbing the camera with one hand, jumping out with (as I recall) the car still in motion, guessing the f-stop—

as the clouds had now obscured the sun—cocking the shutter, checking the focus, removing the slide, aiming and shooting.

The light deteriorated in a hurry, and the afternoon hours were quickly slipping by. A seven-hour drive home was ahead of us and that storm looked ominous. (Eventually, it gave us some five hours driving in the snow.) We broke off the chase and headed south with that ultimate "grab shot" in the film pack.

The moral to this story is when the train is nipping at your heels, it's too late to consult the camera manual.

Later, this photo was published in Kalmbach's *Canadian Steam* by *Trains* magazine's David P. Morgan.

convictions. The authors have their biases too. Brian and John are long-time Nikon users.

John has used Nikon Fs for more than 30 years. In the last 15 years, Brian primarily has used Nikon 35mm SLRs for color, and has experimented with Canons. He also has used Contax and Leica rangefinders, as well as medium format equipment. While these cameras work for us, that doesn't mean they will be the best for you.

Before you settle on one brand or system, look at as many different types of cameras as you can. Ask your friends what they like. find out if a system has notable flaws before you invest in it. Generally, more expensive systems can give you better quality if used skillfully. However, more expensive equipment doesn't insure better photography.

Many professional 35mm format photographers prefer either Canon or Nikon equipment. These durable, flexible systems offer availability and versatility. Visit a camera shop and ask to look at top-end 35mm SLRs, even if you can't afford one now.

Take time to learn about the cameras. Hold one and look through the viewfinder. Discover what makes it worth more than the others. Is it a Ferrari or a Rolls Royce? Is it a GP38 or a TGV? Then look at cheaper models and do the same. If you have a friend who is willing to let you borrow his/her camera, experiment with it. Some professional camera stores, especially those in large cities, offer camera leasing. That will give you the opportunity to try various professional models without an obligation to buy.

Medium Format

Medium format cameras use larger film. That size can provide a larger viewfinder space in which to compose your image, and, most importantly, allows more information on the negative or transparency. That increases the image's tonal richness and allows high-quality enlargements. Medium format cameras permit images of different proportions.

Many medium format cameras, such as a Hasselblad or Rolleiflex, make square images, rather than the typical 1:1.5 ratio offered by most 35mm cameras. Working with a square offers a new composition perspective. Some photographers prefer the square format and have used it to produce spectacular results. Others use the format to print either vertical or rectangular images after exposure.

A short telephoto is an ideal portrait lens. This portrait of rail worker Tom Farance was made early in the morning on Sept. 14, 1977, inside the cab of a Milwaukee Road General Electric-built locomotive at East Rio, Wisconsin.

Photo by John Gruber
Nikon F, 105mm f2.5 Nikkor lens;
Kodachrome 64

Pat Yough prefers the Canon EOS 35mm SLR's superior autofocus system, excellent quality, ease of use and dependability. On July 10, 2002, at 6:07 p.m., Canadian Pacific Railway train No. 505-10 was photographed in The Bronx, New York.

Photo by Patrick Yough
Canon EOS 3; 35mm f2 lens;
Fuji Astia 100 (RAP) exposed @ f6.3 1/640

Consider the weight of a camera system. This photograph was made of a CSX train near Ft. Montgomery, New York. To reach this location requires a one-hour, uphill hike. The photographer used a relatively lightweight 35mm Canon EOS SLR and a zoom lens.

Photo by Tom Mangan
Canon EOS 1V; 70-200mm f2.8 zoom lens;
Fuji Provia 100F (III) exposed @ f6.3 1/640

Many photographers prefer medium format cameras for black and white images. The larger negative size is easier to manipulate in the darkroom. They produce a broader tonal range than is possible with 35mm negatives. Larger negatives require less magnification. The final image suffers less image degradation when it's enlarged for printing or reproduction.

Also, the medium format may be easier to digitally scan, since you can scan a larger negative at lower resolutions and you still have more data to work with in post-processing. Medium format cameras can produce a traditional look that makes them a popular choice for railway photography.

Medium format cameras also come in rangefinder and single-lens reflex models. One popular type of medium format camera is the twin-lens reflex. It's major advantage is no moving mirror.

Choose equipment that allows you to make great images by manipulating basic controls such as shutter speed, aperture, and focus. This time exposure of the North Shore terminal on the Chicago El was made on tripod with existing light.

Photo by Richard Jay Solomon
Kodak Retina IIIC; 50mm f2.0 Schneider lens; Kodachrome

Steve Patterson

"Capture the scene. Be objective. Have a roving eye," says Steve Patterson, a Tennessee native who got his first camera, a Brownie 620, about 1948.

"Ask yourself, 'What is it you want your photograph to do? Is it entertainment or a shot in the dark?'"

When he goes out today to make photographs, it is for fun, recreation, and fellowship. Two other photographers live nearby in Arvada, Colorado. Joe McMillan, a retired Santa Fe employee and friend since the 1950s, has lived next door since 1995. Artist/ photographer Mike Danneman is about two miles away. During a heavy snowstorm, when driving is difficult, he and McMillan make photographs of Amtrak's *California Zephyr* from their back yards.

A slide show at Danneman's home reminded them of an anniversary. He started work for the Santa Fe (now Burlington Northern Santa Fe) 38 years ago, on March 22, 1965.

Since late 1999, he has had a safety job with a regular schedule, rather than being a part of a locomotive engineer's "first in-first out" freight pool. He covers Colorado and western Kansas. As part of a 20-member team, he occasionally may travel to other stations on the BNSF.

"Nobody ever told me trains were meant to be photographed. I just started doing it," he says.

The first camera came when he had a paper route and the newspaper gave them as a bonus for getting new subscribers. When he heard a train, he would hang the camera by its strap over the handlebars of his bicycle, ride six blocks to the Clinchfield tracks, and take a photograph. Most of the photos came back blurry, because of the slow shutter speed. Processing the film cost more than the camera.

Friendships developed at this time continue today. Six charter members of the "Clinchfield Mafia"—all enthusiastic Clinchfield photographers—became acquainted. Patterson reached out farther as the friends turned 16 and could take the 14-year-old in a car with them to make photographs out of town.

He has known McMillan since 1953 or 1954, when he answered a pen pal ad from McMillan, then living in Yorktown, Texas.

Getting started wasn't easy. "I had to learn the hard way. Nobody knows it all; we all have role models. Kids today start with a Nikon. It took us 15-20 years to get a Nikon. Kids today may not even mess with film."

He acquired his first Pentax single lens reflex camera and did color photography for the first time close to his 16th birthday, in 1956.

"At the time, I thought it was the biggest waste I have ever known." Magazines wanted black and white photos. "We took only one frame because of the turn knob film advance, and we were poor. It was a grievous error. Today, I only have one early slide of a scene to work with."

With encouragement from *Trains* editor David P. Morgan, Patterson purchased a good-quality camera to illustrate a Cotton Belt article, published in November 1962. There have been many articles since. Over the years, Patterson went through six Pentax cameras and various lenses until the Pentax repairman told him, "Don't bring that camera in here anymore. We don't have parts for it." He switched to Nikon in December 2001. He still has a Mamiya 645 for black and white, which he hasn't used for several years.

Patterson graduated from East Tennessee State University in December, 1963. It took two years to get the railroad job.

"For a beginning, look at what is out there in calendars, books, and magazines," Patterson advises.

"The first issue of *Trains* (October 1948) had a big impact on me, with an article by Ward Kimball, who rode a cab forward over Tehachapi Pass at night with an engineer who was making his last run. The seed was planted. We corresponded about that some 43 years later when I was an engineer."

"See what gets published," he concludes. "Recognize what is out there. Start getting original. Decide what you would like to portray. Develop your own styles and objectives. It's fun."

On Feb. 2, 1965, Clinchfield's only FP7 (no. 200) and a pair of F7bs cross the south fork of Holston River into Kingsport, Tennessee, in 10 inches of snow. Steve Patterson bought a used Speed Graphic for $150 and took this photo with his "advanced" camera.

Photo by Steve Patterson
Speed Graphic; Kodak Royal Pan Film exposed @ f16 1/400th with yellow K2 filter

Many 120 film cameras produce 60 x 60mm (2 inch) square negatives. This size and format has been used successfully for railway photography and is a good choice for black and white. This view of Irish Rail was made with a Rolleiflex at Killiney Co., Dublin, overlooking the Irish Sea.

Photo by Brian Solomon
Rolleiflex T; 75mm f3.5 Zeiss Tessar lens; Ilford HP-5 400 ASA (rated at 200) processed in Ilford ID-11 1:1 with water for seven minutes at 68 degrees F, with two minute pre-wash; printed on Agfa Classic FB glossy.

This reduces mechanical complexity and requires less repair and maintenance. The camera's weight and motion is reduced, increasing the potential for sharper pictures.

Rolleiflex and Mamiya are among the better known manufacturers of twin-lens reflexes. A disadvantage is, without the aid of a prism, the viewfinder displays a mirror image. Composing photos backward takes a bit of practice.

Many types of medium format single-lens reflex cameras, like the Hasselblad and Bronica, use interchangeable film backs. This allows a photographer to use a single body with various types of film without having to replace a roll of film prematurely.

For many years, medium format and large format "press cameras," such as the Speed Graphic and 4x5 SLR Graflex, were used by railroad photographers. Essentially, these are portable versions of a view camera designed for action photography. Some of these retained modified tilts and swings that allowed for perspective correction. They incorporated other features that made rail photos easier, such as rangefinders or improved viewfinders, focal-plane

shutters, multi-pack sheet film backs, and bellows on a folding track. While press cameras may seem difficult and unwieldy to use, they were the tools of choice for many great railroad photographers over the years.

Improved camera technology hasn't necessarily resulted in better images. Look at the best work of

Phil Hastings, Jim Shaughnessy, Lucius Beebe, and Richard Steinheimer from the 1940s and '50s and decide for yourself.

Disadvantages to larger format cameras are they tend to be bulkier and heavier than 35mm equipment. Generally, they require more skill to operate. Many medium format cameras aren't equipped with

The square format can be used to great advantage. It allows distinctive compositions such as this December 1999 view of an Irish Rail empty sugar beet train rolling along the River Suir at Bellview in Waterford, Ireland.

Photo by Brian Solomon

Rolleiflex T; 75mm f3.5 Zeiss Tessar lens; Ilford HP-5 400 ASA (rated at 200) processed in Ilford ID-11 1:1 with water for seven minutes at 68 degrees F, with two minute pre-wash; printed on Agfa Classic FB glossy.

New Haven's No. 177 *The Senator* passes Sharon, Massachusetts, led by 4-6-4 Shoreliner type 1402, on November 21, 1941. George C. Corey says: "In a little over two weeks, Pearl Harbor would be attacked and my innocent world, as well as everybody else's, would be changed forever. Among the changes would be no more photographs along the railroads for the duration of the war. Photographically, considering I was 16 years of age at the time, I think the picture is quite good. The camera I had at the time had a top shutter speed of 1/150th of a second, hardly adequate by contemporary standards, but which seems to have stopped the action pretty well. I actually took my first railroad photograph in 1934, but didn't really get hooked until 1938. By 1941, I was doing fairly well, but the four years of the war slowed down the learning process."

Photo by George C. Corey

easy-to-use features such as autofocus, auto exposure modes, and built-in meters.

Medium format lenses tend to be slower than those used by 35mm cameras, so it can be more difficult to shoot moving trains with high shutter speeds. Longer, physically larger lenses are required to cover the film size. A normal lens with a camera that uses 120 size 2 1/4 square film will be 75 to 80mm, rather than 45 to 50mm on a 35mm format camera. Longer lenses result in shallower depth of field and greater blurring from camera motion.

The primary disadvantages to new medium format compared to 35mm equipment is their cost. Film is much more costly per frame and may be

David and Jill Oroszi

"You don't have to go to all the exotic places that you see in the magazines to get good pictures. There are good opportunities in your back yard," advises David Oroszi. "Although I like to travel around the country, I have done tons of stuff in my own back yard, my own area around Dayton, Ohio, for 35 years."

"I feel compelled to record history, but it's just plain fun to take railroad photographs and it gets me outside. It is an excuse to go to many different places and it is a great way to combine my interest in the outdoors, trains, and photography."

With others, he echoes the need for newcomers to learn the basics.

"I always try to make sure people understand the need to master the 50mm lens and the camera first. Too many people get too enthusiastic, don't understand when to use certain lenses, and how to use light. To develop your own style, see what other people are doing. Go to multi-media shows like SummeRail, Eastrail and WinteRail. Subscribe to magazines. Figure out what you like and don't like. Please yourself."

Oroszi was fortunate to have help from older Dayton-area photographers, like Alvin Schultze and Charles Mockbee, when he was starting out in the 1960s. In turn, he now helps younger photographers get started whenever he can.

Although Dave was a typical kid in the 1950s, he grew up with a strong appreciation of both art and music.

"In grade school, I attended art classes at the Dayton Art Institute and primarily did paintings and drawings. I also enjoyed music and sang in various choirs. Then in high school in the 1960s, I was focused on music as a bass guitarist in a rock-and-roll band. In 1967, I met Jill, my wife of over 30 years, one night when my rock-and-roll band was playing at a local dance." Later that same year, while attending his first year of college, his childhood interest in trains was rekindled, which evolved into an interest in railroad photography he has been pursuing ever since.

Eventually, Dave was able to combine his interest in photography and music by producing multimedia shows and becoming one of the main organizers of SummeRail at Cincinnati Union Terminal.

The first photography attempts were mostly 50mm "wedgie" action and roster type shots, starting with an Instamatic. He got his first 35mm camera in the spring of 1969. It wasn't until after being exposed to *CTC Board* magazine and multimedia WinteRail shows in the late-1980s that he started expanding his types of photographs to include a more artsy approach including signs, people, interiors, low light, storms, and so forth.

Rather than taking random shots around the country, Oroszi likes to document railroad lines. He includes all possible aspects of the railroad. He's not overly interested in types of locomotives or roster photography, but still likes to have clean locomotives to photograph. His first away-from-home project was the B&O and Eire Lackawanna in the mid-1970s. Then he moved on to the Frisco and L&N.

On the L&N, which included coverage of almost the entire railroad, he got involved with the L&N Historical Society and started meeting people away from the Dayton area. He then spent about three years documenting the Southern, about 10 years following the Santa Fe, three years on the C&NW and UP, five to six years on the SP, and a couple years on the Wisconsin Central, just before it was sold.

He photographs stations, structures, and people. His one regret is he didn't photograph railroaders until more recently.

Because of friendships developed over his 35 years in the hobby, he has 14 photo collections in addition to his own, totaling about one million slides and negatives. Many of the photos date back into the 1950s and earlier. He and his wife, Jill, have taken about half of the photographs. They have contributed to all kinds of projects (including eight co-authored books) and helped many others with books, magazine publishing, and articles.

When you talk about Dave, you also must talk about his wife, Jill. Even before they were married, she accompanied him on just about all photography trips. She still does to this day. From the early 1970s until the mid-1990s, Jill took the black and white photographs and Dave specialized in slides.

When the sun goes down and/or clouds appear I rarely "run for the hills." I usually hang around to the last minute, just in case something dramatic happens—sometimes it does, and sometimes it doesn't. On this day in July 2000, a friend and I were following this train south towards home on the CSX Toledo-Cincinnati mainline, south of Columbus Grove, Ohio, after a long day of photography. The skies parted for a moment and I was able to capture the train, framed with some good Ohio corn. The film was Fuji Astia 100 and the exposure was probably 1/500 at f5.6, using a 28mm wide angle lens.

Photo by David P. Oroszi

Initially, they started taking black and whites since most magazines then had little use for color photographs. It was much easier to get black and white published. For a while, he used a mount made by his toolmaker father-in-law, so he could shoot two cameras at once, when Jill wasn't around to take the black and whites.

Today, he has no way of knowing which pictures she took and which ones he did, so many of the black and white photo credits also will include Jill's name. They stopped taking black and whites, mostly because the work of developing and filing was starting to take up too much time.

Oroszi spent 30 years as a computer programmer and information systems analyst, primarily for insurance companies. He headed into semi-retirement in 1999. His familiarity with computers would seem to make the transition to digital photography a natural progression for him. He still takes photographs using slide film. Oroszi acquired a slide scanner in 2002. He calls the computer, scanner, and printer "the darkroom of the day" and hopes to replace the chemical darkroom in the basement with this equipment.

Currently, he is scanning slides, color negatives, and black and white negatives for publishing projects. And he is making computer prints to fulfill requests for large numbers of prints. Dave also expects to use the high-resolution slide scans so originals don't have to be sent to a publisher.

Oroszi learned the basics early on. Today he is reaping the rewards of those careful beginnings.

harder to find locally. High quality medium format cameras may be purchased second hand, which is more economical than buying them new.

Choosing Lenses

There are even greater varieties of lenses than cameras. Camera manufacturers typically offer a range of lenses, including fixed focal length 'primes' from super-wide angle to extreme telephoto, as well as zoom lenses in various lengths. Several systems are noted for their exceptional lenses. Among the highest rated are those made by Leica, Carl Zeiss (used by Contax, Rolleiflex and Hassleblad, and others), Canon and Nikon.

Are these high-end lenses better? In most cases, yes. In comparison with their less-expensive counterparts, high-quality lenses usually are noticeably sharper, use better color coatings, are freer from optical defects, are better made and more durable, and tend to offer wider apertures. This makes them "faster." New top-end lenses typically are very expensive and may be well out of reach for many railway photographers. Top-end lenses can cost three to four times more than comparable consumer-line lenses of the same focal length. Check prices of clean, used lenses—a way to get good, reasonably priced optics.

Beware! Brand name alone isn't necessarily an indication of quality. Some manufacturers produce several different lens lines. Others are noted for making excellent lenses at some focal lengths, but not others. Just because Nikon makes one of the best 105mm telephotos on the market doesn't mean its f1.8 50mm is the same quality.

Sometimes high-end lenses can be distinguished by their lowest f-stop. If a manufacturer offers two 50mm lenses, the f1.4 lens will be more expensive, and probably better quality, than the f2.0. This is especially true with zoom lenses. A relatively slow zoom (f4.5) will be

aimed at the consumer market, while the f2.8 zoom in the same range will be directed at the professional market.

Depending on the manufacturer, quality differences between lines can be minor or extreme. The best way to determine lens quality is to experiment with one. Before buying an expensive lens, you may wish to rent or borrow one from a friend.

Not all lenses are created equal. Lenses of the same model, make, and focal length can vary considerably in their quality. Picky photographers may try dozens of different lenses before they find a really good one. Let your results determine the quality of the lens, not price or reputation.

Fixed versus Zoom Lenses

A zoom is a variable focal length lens. The primary advantage of a zoom lens is convenience. A zoom provides flexibility to fit the scene you are photographing. With modern autofocus cameras, you may be able to zoom out, then gradually pull back, following a moving train. This gives you a variety of photographic opportunities without needing to change lenses or use multiple camera bodies fitted with different focal length lenses.

Using a zoom can reduce the amount of weight you carry, and limit the number of tools you need. The down side of zooms is that you may sacrifice quality for convenience. Some high-end zooms can nearly match the characteristics of fixed lenses. Generally, fixed lenses are faster, sharper, and more durable than zooms.

A zoom has an inherent disadvantage because it requires more elements than a fixed lens. This can result in excessive flare in back-lit situations as well as the "ghosting" of bright light sources included in a photo, such as headlights and the sun. Zooms have moving parts that are more prone to failure and lose critical sharpness when used frequently.

You are better off choosing zoom lenses with a

▲ This sequence portrays an eastbound Conrail intermodal train at Muddy Pond in Hinsdale, Massachusetts, just east of Washington Summit on the old Boston & Albany route, in April 1995. These were made with a Pentax 6 x 7 120 camera—a 120 size SLR that resembles smaller 35mm SLRs in appearance and function.

Photo by Michael Gardner
Pentax 6 x 7; 200mm f4;
Professional Kodachrome 64

Middle: Conrail SD80MACs on the old Boston & Albany, east of Palmer, Massachusetts, near CP79. Using 120 film to produce a square is a popular format with many professional photographers. This photo is reproduced full frame and actual size.

Photo by Michael Gardner
Hasselblad 201F; 80mm f2.8 Zeiss
Planar lens; Fuji Astia 100 (RAP); f5.6 1/500

Bottom: A Utah Railway unit coal train in bright sun at Thistle, Utah, in October 1999. The 645 image size is one of several common medium formats available using 120 and 220 film. This photo demonstrates the actual size of a processed 645 slide—6 x 4.5 cm.

Photo by Michael Gardner
Hasselblad 201F; 120mm f4 Zeiss Makro-Planar
Cfi lens; Ektachrome 100 (EPN); F5.6 1/500

narrower range.

A 28mm to 300mm zoom won't be as high quality as either a 28 to 35mm or 80 to 200mm. The wide focal length range sacrifices convenience over quality. Many consumer zooms feature relatively high minimum apertures. A zoom with an f5.6 minimum will prove limiting, especially in low light. If you are planning to make night photographs, choose faster, more compact lenses.

Perhaps a final consideration is the most important one. A zoom lens can make you lazy. Rather than hunting for exactly the right spot to make the most dramatic photography, a zoom may allow you to get by with an adequate, though substandard view. The handicap of using fixed lenses can make you a more proficient and skilled photographer.

Railway Photographers Paradox

Railway photographers suffer from a time-versus-skill paradox. As skill improves, the railway appears to become less interesting. This leads to inevitable laments like: "How I wish my early photos were better!" And, "If I only knew then, what I know now!"

The paradox seems true, whether you started making photos in 1934 or seven minutes ago. As you learn photography, your aptitude for it improves. This means your earliest photos will be your least-skilled attempts. Many railway photographers are drawn to their subject because they want to preserve an element of the railway before it disappears.

Perhaps a favorite line is about to be abandoned, or classic locomotives are facing retirement. Mergers, resignalling projects and loss of passenger services all are events that have propelled railway photographers into action.

Looking back, you may be frustrated reviewing your earliest images. To you, the subject was at its most interesting, yet your ability to capture it was at its least developed state.

Lest H.G. Wells' time machine makes its appearance, you can't go back. Your best alternative is to refine your photography skills for the future. Learn what you need to know, and practice. Some photographers are fast learners who quickly pick up the basics. Others may need remedial help. If you're just starting out, several things can help you jump-start your efforts.

- Keep your mind open and be willing to try different equipment and techniques.
- Vary your images.
- Master the use of your tools.
- See light and learn to make it work for you.
- Keep detailed notes so you can learn from both successes and failures.
- Analyze your results critically and often. Accept your failures and avoid repeating them. Denial of failure is a dangerous trap.
- Listen to criticism and use it to improve your techniques. Don't invent excuses to validate poor skills or to justify continued use of defective equipment.
- Replace or repair defective equipment right away. Don't be caught out by something you know doesn't work properly.
- Use high quality materials. There is no savings in using poor quality film.
- Use the very best cameras and lenses you can afford.
- Recognize quality when you see it.
- Ask questions and learn from your peers.
- Anticipate changes on the railways you photograph. Careful attention to detail can alert you to the inevitable metamorphosis of your favorite railway(s).
- Don't delay making photographs until changes make your efforts difficult or nearly impossible. Get started as soon as possible. In time, everything will change. Today's common scene will someday seem unusual, and photos of it will be precious.
- Don't allow change to discourage your photography.
- Keep at it, don't be lazy, and enjoy yourself!

In October 1956, Norfolk & Western's westbound train No. 5 crosses a steel trestle near Coeburn, Virginia. Steve Patterson says: "This photo was made with a 127-size film camera using drug store Verichrome pan. The object here is, you knew the train's schedule, you selected a primo spot to capture it. It was about purpose, pursuit, and product." By modern standards, the technical quality may not seem high, but this is a fantastic photo. You can feel the young photographer's enthusiasm.

Photo by Steve Patterson
Kodak Verichrome Pan exposed 1/50 ▷

By Richard Jay Solomon

CHAPTER 3

DIGITAL PHOTOGRAPHY

◀

Former Milwaukee Road Alco-built Northern No. 261 in steam at its Minneapolis home in May 2000. A 1.5 Megapixel Nikon in overcast light, auto exposure with zoom lens at wide-angle. Light post-processing. Image sent to printer for color-separation at 300 dpi.

Photo by Richard Jay Solomon
Nikon 900, Nikkor 5.8-17.4mm zoom lens, auto exposure, flash off

✳ Revolutions in photography have arrived in just about every generation since its invention in the 1830s. The last time photography went through a radical shift was between 1950 and the mid-1960s with the introduction of 35mm cameras and faster, finer-grain color films.

This was also the era when diesel locomotives replaced steam. There was enough overlap so the last of steam was captured in color with high-resolution, action photography.

It is no coincidence that we are in another technological revolution today with digital electronics impacting just about everything—from washing machines to diesel engines. It shouldn't come as a surprise that photography is changing, too.

It's not as novel as it may seem. Electronics started changing photography about 20 years ago with the introduction of automatic exposure control, automatic focusing, and rapid frame advance. These advances eased the average rail photographer's ability to capture a rapidly moving scene with less fuss.

Skilled practitioners using color film, such as Don Ball, had mastered those details much earlier, using manual techniques in the early 1950s in a period when rail fan pros like Steinheimer, Link, Beebe, Clegg, Hastings, Plowden, Shaughnessy, and others continued to use medium- and large-format press cameras for their quality black-and-white action photos.

By the 1980s, with the widespread use of automation, even amateurs, were shooting credible images with much less skill. Use of digital electronics in the period lowered the cost of screened separations for printing and allowed color photographs to be published more readily. In the 1950s and '60s, color rarely was found in railroad magazines or books. Many photographers were discouraged from shooting in color.

The evolutionary changes in film rail photography that early electronics stimulated should forecast what's to come with all-digital imaging. In the 1970s, electronics altered publications with many niche rail fan magazines and books appearing.

For the first time, many publications had decent color reproduction, documenting activities and scenes that rarely had appeared outside of short-lived club slide shows and private collections that had only been seen by a small circle of friends. Overall technical quality and broader subject coverage improved, though artistic ability was lacking.

Cheap photolithography in the 1950s meant that most pictures were badly reproduced. Even well-composed shots were muddy and indistinct—the rare exceptions being *Trains* magazine and Central Electric Railfans Assn. and National Historical Railway Society publications. Few of these were worth preserving for their photos, many were thrown away. Today, rare specimens sell for exorbitant prices on eBay. With electronic imaging, the future may see more online, CD, and DVD sources than paper publications.

Lessons in Digital Photography

Please note that resolution, color correction and color gamut

The cab of Milwaukee Road 261 with the sky completely overcast, shot with medium telephoto. The digital camera captures the black and red quite well, automatically compensating exposure for the completely overcast sky. No post-processing.

Photo by Richard Jay Solomon
Nikon 900, Nikkor 5.8-17.4mm zoom lens, auto exposure

(the range of color) are as important for digital image quality as they are with film image quality.

One problem with the previous film revolution—which digital is in danger of repeating—was that color larger than 35mm was too expensive for amateur photographers. That made it difficult to satisfactorily produce really large prints—which demand high quality for large images.

Future generations may expect better results than those we currently produce with most digital cameras. Film may have reached a zenith in resolving power but we're not close with electronics.

Comparisons aren't simple. A digital photograph equivalent to the sharpest, properly exposed 35mm slide, using the best quality lens (such as a Leica Summicron) with no camera shake would contain 30 to 40 megapixels.

With the exception of expensive, high-end professional studio devices, digital cameras range from below one megapixel (one million "picture elements") to around six megapixels.

The best small format professional electronic digital SLR, hand-held cameras today are only about 11 to 13 megapixels. They cost as much as $8,000-$10,000 (though prices are coming down). Some photographers feel they barely approach the color gamut or luminance ratio (the measurable amount of light emitted or reflected from a source) of today's best films. Medium format film resolution is about four times that of 35mm, and large format (4 x 5" or more) is 10 to 20 times greater!

Digital photography also has other tradeoffs besides resolving power, color, and gamma functions between electronics and film. Today's digital technology simply isn't good enough to reproduce all the colors or equal the resolution and luminance gamma of film.

The ultimate result of your photography is how you expect to view or display your pictures—today and in the future.

It's easy to predict displays will be huge in the future. Homes soon will have five-foot diagonal, high-definition video screens. Such large screens already are common with electronic projectors used in corporations and classrooms. At that size, even 11 megapixels look substandard compared to 35mm projected slides.

Comparisons also must include the digital "bit depth" for sampling the color "gamut." That's the total span of colors that can be captured. (The digital standard of 36 bits of color per pixel, barely approaches the equivalent of color transparencies.) Even the professional and pro-sumer (those one step below the professional models but above consumer models) cannot compare with the best color films.

Unlike film, most digital sensors are linear, and use complex formulae to compensate. That may not produce the satisfactory results of film, though you have a better chance to succeed with more expensive digital cameras.

The best digital cameras are incapable of capturing the deep purples, darker reds, and the brighter greens. And dependable color photo reproduction on a Web page is pretty much nil. All television displays, even HDTV, are worse than most computer monitors.

Opposite Page: Maximum resolution with digital output for post processing can be better than film alone. The Köln, Germany, Hauptbahnhof (main station) was shot in October 2002 on Fuji Provia F film with a Leica lens, scanned at 4000 lines per inch. A 54 Megabyte TIFF file was processed with Photoshop on a Macintosh G4 to lighten areas and correct color cast. Inset is magnified 24x.

Photo by Richard Jay Solomon
Leica M4, 35mm f1.4 Leitz Summilux lens, Fuji Provia 100 F (RDP III) scanned on Polaroid 4000

Amtrak's New Haven-Springfield shuttle at Berlin, Connecticut, in September 2002, shot on a Nikon 3.5 Megapixel camera, with Photoshop post-processing to lighten the front of the Genesis engine and capture the cumulus clouds.

Photo by Richard Jay Solomon
Nikon 885, Nikkor zoom lens set normal, auto exposure

Tiny electronic cameras shoot good pictures—if you don't enlarge them. Amtrak's Acela at the Newark Airport station was taken at VGA resolution (640 x 480 pixels). This shot is as big as it can get without falling into digital artifacts—a fine shot for e-mail or the Web.

Photo by Richard Jay Solomon
Che-ez by SpyZ

Digital Role in Railroad Photography

In my professional life, I design extremely high-resolution, super-color-gamut, high-frame-rate digital video systems for science, military, and medical applications. Yet, I carry my 35mm Leica film cameras for *important* subjects—such as railroads!

Digital has a role in railroad photography and is worth exploring because *it will get better*. If your goal is making prints not much larger than 8 x 10," almost any three-megapixel digital camera in the $500-$1,000 range will do.

One advantage of a non-SLR digital camera is the lack of mirror bounce, which helps produce sharper pictures, especially with slow shutter speeds.

You may find that for low-light or night rail photography, with little or no train motion, a medium-priced digital camera is easier to work with than pushing film, choosing filters, or hand-holding a bulky SLR.

Digital has no reciprocity failure which can be very helpful in night photography—though digital has trouble interpreting data in low light situations.

As with modern film cameras, automation takes care of most photo parameters, even in extreme lighting circumstances or with rapidly-moving objects—*as long as you read the manual.*

Automatic focusing on some higher-end digital cameras allows you to take a rapid succession of images and you can choose the sharpest or best-exposed for storage.

If all you care about is a small image for your Internet Web site, you can get away with much less camera. I often carry the SpyZ "Che-ez" electronic camera—no bigger than a matchbook. It takes perfectly good small photos for e-mail and is fine for grabbing them without attracting attention. The pictures look best in their matchbook size.

As image sensors become more miniaturized and processing software is more sophisticated, such cameras will be built into all sorts of other hand-held devices.

Electronic photography brings the ability to see your photos almost instantly. The feedback teaches you to make better pictures—or correct mistakes—faster.

Coupled with computers, it offers a larger set of imaging options. These options include variable low-light sensitivity and easier manipulation of color balance or color correction for difficult lighting, such as fluorescent lights or arc lamps.

Storage capacity isn't constrained by the 12 to 36 exposure film length. It can be hundreds of shots, just like a movie, depending on what you are using for storage media.

For rapidly-moving trains, dim illumination, strange environments, or the need to see your pictures right away, digital can be a major advantage. Manipulating light and color in night photography and seeing whether you got anything at all is critical.

A key problem, even with the expensive, professional digital cameras, is an annoying delay from the time the camera is powered until you can shoot. There is a further delay in downloading an electronic image to storage.

Digital is less handy for static scenery, good lighting, stations, interiors on a tripod, idle engines, and super-resolution archival views. The price to pay with digital often includes a bulky device, expensive batteries, and complex storage media. And there are few compatibility standards among the important accessories.

You should consider the significant benefits of electronic imaging. One is you can forget the darkroom and those carcinogenic chemicals for color processing. Printing and image manipulation now is done using the computer.

Image manipulation today has become easy for even a rank amateur. Everything from altering color to engine details and faking backgrounds and foregrounds can be applied readily, without much skill. With expertise, it is hardly detectable.

We must accept that pictures no longer are evidence of historical facts. Not only digitally-exposed images, but any past photograph that is electronically scanned can be manipulated. Few archivists want to face this issue, but it is real and threatens future historical narratives.

Electronics does not yet mean the end of film. More likely, both can and will co-exist for some time, with interesting synergies. High-quality film scanners have become very cheap, making it possible to digitize archives and apply very sophisticated software to restore and enhance old photographs.

Today, modern scanners allow photographers to continue to use film for the highest resolution (and maximum portability), yet capture virtually all of the filmed characteristics for further computer manipulation.

Digital photography is a work in progress. You'll see many changes over the next few years. As with most computerized equipment, devices will become obsolete faster than your bank account will appreciate. You have to acquire things judiciously, as prices will drop and features will continually expand. Expect changes at least once a year.

Storage Issues

Eventually, electronics will replace and exceed today's best films. Every photographer can instantly be an Internet publisher, creating an explosion of rail photographs. Storage and retrieval already have become major problems. Archival standards are nonexistent.

Black and white film may last for many years if processed and stored properly. Some color transparencies may last hundreds of years under pristine conditions. Yet color negative film, paper prints, magnetic tape, and CDs and DVDs may have a relatively short lifespan.

It's important to understand the differences in CD quality. Professional CDs cost around 5 cents apiece,

Milwaukee Road's Skytop Lounge observation car from its old Hiawatha passenger trains, shot with an electronic camera in May 2000 at Minneapolis Jct. Color correction in Photoshop can fix an orange cast created by the built-in camera's auto-color feature.

Photo by Richard Jay Solomon
Nikon 900, Zoom Nikkor 5.8-17.4mm lens, auto exposure

but machines for duplication cost up to $1 million. Such CDs are reasonably robust if fungus doesn't get below the plastic and the surface isn't scratched. CDs you make at home can cost from 29 cents to $3 or $4 each and have very short lifetimes.

More expensive CD blanks may last decades, assuming they're carefully stored and infrequently played. If you go the CD route, make at least three copies.

DVDs you make yourself are even more fragile. Instead of the laser beam drilling microscopic pits, they create interference patterns on the surface. These patterns are even tinier and less robust.

Merely digitizing and recopying every few decades is no solution since the costs will be prohibitive to duplicate bits over and over again. Another problem would be to find a machine—say, 50 years from now—that would recognize the data format or the CD itself.

One solution for images intended for archiving might be to print them onto film, even if they originated electronically. Then store the film in zero-humidity freezers, though that's not exactly a convenient means for accessibility.

It may just be, despite the high technology of our 21st century, the only railroad photos that will be around in, say, the 31st century will be glass plates of steam locomotive builders from the 19th century. Will today's diesels and electrics be totally forgotten?

Just the simple task of sorting digital images for a magazine editor, a presentation, or your own files still is difficult compared to transparencies. Sorting software isn't yet fast enough or simple enough to compete with popping a few dozen slides from a box on a light table.

That assumes you even know what is in the "electronic box" where you file your digital images.

With a slide, a good art director who uses a loupe can tell almost immediately whether the slide will reproduce well. A printer can tell what the col-

Amtrak GENESIS engine idling at Springfield, Massachusetts, on February 20, 2003. An easy picture for a 1.5 megapixel digital camera to expose. No post processing needed.

Photo by Richard Jay Solomon
Nikon 900, Zoom Nikkor 5.8-17.4mm lens, auto exposure

ors and balance should be. All of this will be feasible, and potentially superior, with digital images, but the skills and software have yet to be perfected.

Recommendations

Here are some practical recommendations for the rail photographer who wants to take the digital plunge.

First, don't throw away all your film equipment or your photographs. Start with an easy transition, like scanning your slides and negatives.

Scanners require software. Some of the bundled variety is excellent, but your criteria should be how easy it is to use. Most software can be tested before you commit.

If your primary interest is archival scanning, it's best to set your high-end scanner on "raw," and on the highest spatial and color resolution. This will capture the full amount of data in the slide or negative, though you might not see good screen images.

After "raw scanning," most pros use Adobe Photoshop. It's neither cheap nor easy, but is full of wonderful features that allow sophisticated modification.

Unless you only intend to view your digital photos on a computer monitor or projector, you will need a printer. Inexpensive inkjet printers cost from $80 to $200 and are excellent for up to 8 x 10" prints. Prints can appear as good as anything sent to photo labs. For about twice that price you can get printers that use archival inks.

The bad news is ink cartridges can get very expensive and inkjet prints are no cheaper than conventional photosensitive prints. An alternative is to bring or transmit your digital media to a service bureau for printing.

The last recommendation is about buying a digital camera. If you gradually move into digital via film scanning and printing, you should gain an appreciation of what fits your budget and photo style.

If you have existing film equipment, a comfortable transition would be a digital body that uses your current lenses.

An alternative is to get a $300-$400, three megapixel, point-and-shoot camera and use both film and electronics. This will give you experience with digital features and problems, such as picture delay, batteries, and choice of storage media.

You'll indulge in a never-ending suite of accessories including a range of storage media, lenses, and filters designed for digital sensors, remote control devices, and various special uses software. The future is infinite.

Considering that immense changes are still to come, digital electronics will offer a wider palette for rail fan photographers. The artist can be even more creative. Publication now is instantaneous and global, via the World Wide Web.

Hopefully, we'll find some way to preserve all these images and maintain an interest in railroads and railroad archives for all time.

Pros and Cons of Digital from a Profession Perspective
by Steve Smedley

I am a staff photojournalist for *The Pantagraph*, one of Central Illinois' largest newspapers. The switch from film to digital has been a huge technical leap and has greatly simplified image production.

In a typical scenario, I'm sitting in the warmth of my vehicle, radio scanners reporting slick roads and vehicle accidents. On the passenger seat are two camera bags. Inside are two Nikon D1H cameras, one with a 20-35 2.8 zoom, and the other with a Nikon 80-200mm zoom. My "films" are two Lexar Media Compact-Flash cards.

The 256MB cards are equal to about four rolls of 36-exposure film and one 24-exposure roll. They are considered old in this ever-changing digital environment, rated at 10X in terms of the ability of the cards to process images to memory.

My cards can be set for a 200 to 1600 ISO, in normal camera settings. While the D1H allows a setting to a higher ISO, I don't use them due to the high "noise" (grain) level associated with the higher speeds.

Behind me is a Pelican case with a Mac Powerbook, equipped with Photo Mechanic Lite, and Adobe Photoshop 6.0. A cell phone adapter, card reader and extra cords are all I need to send photos via phone and modem to our paper's computer photo archive. The weakest link is the cell phone signal in rural areas.

Several years ago, I was sent to digital technology seminars—technical boot camps. I learned to scan film negatives into digital computer files. The final turn for me was being issued two Kodak DCS 760 digital cameras, based on Nikon F5 bodies. These cameras are cumbersome, and that's a compliment! They were replaced with new Nikon D1H cameras and lens sets.

I welcomed the switch to digital media since I shoot everything from late-breaking news to sporting events. Imagine doing this on a tight deadline, then driving back to the newspaper office—sometimes 50 to 60 miles away. Digital is much simpler.

Back in the days when we used film, a complicating factor was the need to make several separate processing runs to accommodate various film speeds. I'd often change film types for each assignment.

I still prefer using slides for personal work, trading them with fellow fans, submitting them for publication, and being able to throw together a two-projector show.

I am not ready to stop shooting slide film for my railroad photography. Slides will be my medium for the next several years. The present quality limitations of digital compared to film are the primary reason I prefer to stick with film for now. It's hard to tell the difference between 8x10 prints made from a slide and those from D1H digital file—if the prints have been done properly.

I can imagine being able to move current rail-related news photos and events to a personal Web site in the future. Perhaps there will be CD shows, where a photographer's work is shown during the same hour it is made. The possibilities are exciting, but I am sticking with the little cassettes of film.

The technology is developing so quickly, it worries me that in 10 to 15 years I might not be able to read the CD-Rs used for storing digital images. I would rather have my original slides in some railroad historical society collection, than on a disc.

Someday, maybe we will sit down to a high-quality all-digital railroad slide show. But not just yet.

CHAPTER 4

TECHNIQUE & COMPOSITION

◀

✳ This chapter is about seeing and composing images and different techniques you can try. Ask yourself questions when you photograph. How can you divide your frame? What elements should you include and exclude? Do you compose your frame in advance with your camera carefully positioned on a tripod, or do you go for the grab shot, and arrange your photo on the fly?

The Whole Scene

When you compose, observe the entire scene, not just the railroad or a specific train. Look at all the elements. Watch for those that may give a photo added interest. Railway structures, scenery, signaling, and people all can contribute to a photograph. Work with various elements to make a balanced composition and keep a keen eye for distracting elements that might disrupt or spoil your image.

Watch your foreground, carefully avoiding unsightly elements that may detract from the shot. A beautiful scene with a train rolling across a field against a background of purple mountains can be spoiled by a bit of litter in the foreground.

When you work tight to the tracks, watch for mounds of ballast and stray ties left over from the last big maintenance project. If railroad maintenance still is going on, look for welded rail, tie piles, and spike buckets. These elements can be used to tell a story if they're carefully placed. When badly placed, they detract from good composition.

Look around. Are there flowers or fresh green grass? Bend down or kneel and observe. As you get low, use a wide angle lens and place flowers, grass and other objects in the foreground to produce a more colorful photo.

Mind the subjects of your image. What are you photographing? A scene, a building, a locomotive, or a train? Too many elements can result in a cluttered image. If you can't use an element to your advantage, minimize it, or better, crop it out.

Poles and Wires

Badly placed poles and wires can scar an otherwise perfect scene. A pole line can be the bane of clean composition. Carefully place the front of the locomotive between the poles. Avoid unsightly, distracting intersections. Be equally aware if a pole line runs behind the tracks. If you aren't careful, poles may seem to protrude like alien antennas. High tension lines flowing through the sky without any obvious means of support can seem like scratches. Yet, by making use of pole

lines and wires, a potential distraction can be made into a desirable element that holds the whole composition together.

Lens, Sky, and Vantage Point

When you select a lens, see how it affects your background and foreground. A wide-angle lens can be used to include more foreground and telephoto lens for less. If unpleasant foreground elements cause you grief, try a long telephoto and a wide aperture. The foreground will fall into a sea of blur which may minimize the distraction.

By contrast, if there are rows of unsightly high-tension lines, modern highway bridges, or other such intrusions in the distance, try using a wide-angle lens to minimize the background.

A telephoto lens will draw these elements in, but a wide-angle lens can be used to make them seem farther away and less obtrusive. If you want to emphasize high-tension towers, try using a long

Poppies make a textured foreground in this April 9, 1994 photo of California Northern's GP15-1 at Petaluma. This low-angle view was made in bright sun with a 28mm wide-angle lens. A high depth of field puts all elements of the image in relative focus.

Photo by Brian Solomon
**Nikon F3T; 28mm f2.8 Nikkor AF lens;
Kodachrome 25 exposed @ f11 1/60**

Opposite Page: Light and shadow define all photographic images. This view was made at 9:45 a.m. on Nov. 7, 1987 in the Natural Tunnel on the former Southern Railway, north of Clinchport, Virginia. The CSX train's headlight is crucial to the whole composition.

Photo by J. D. Schmid
**Nikon F3; 35mm PC Nikkor lens;
Kodachrome 25**

telephoto lens in a vertical format to capture the train passing between the towers, with them marching off to the horizon like an army of soldiers.

Should you include the sky or crop it out? When there is a clear blue dome, you may wish to keep it in. On a dull cloudy day, when a slate-gray sky prevails that adds nothing to the image, crop it! A bit of elevation can help minimize a dull sky. Work from an overhead bridge, or the top of an embankment.

Often, at sunset the sky opens to reveal a complex pattern of interweaving clouds. Feature the sky, work with the cloud patterns and make them part of your composition.

You can make a more compelling image if you give a little more emphasis to either the sky or the foreground. Avoid splitting the difference by putting the horizon exactly in the middle. Once in awhile, an even horizon can be used to produce a strong and rigidly-balanced image. If you do this too often, the technique may result in bland images. So watch your horizon and make the most of it!

Working with Light and Shadow

Always keep an eye on lighting. The quality of light can make or break a composition. Heavy clouds result in flat, directionless light that is unflattering and bland. High sun produces bright, harsh, high-contrast light that is difficult to work with. Low morning or afternoon sun is among the best light. Keep an eye on shadows.

▷

Shadows frame Pennsylvania Railroad MP54 multiple units seen at 52nd St. Overbrook Station near Philadelphia, Pennsylvania, in the winter of 1962.

Photo by Richard Jay Solomon
Leica M3; 50mm f2 Summicron lens; Kodachrome II

Poles and wires make distracting shadows. When you're shooting a moving train, watch where the shadows fall and avoid allowing the front of the engine to intersect shadows in ways that cause undesirable line convergence.

In bright sun, watch for reflections that may be distracting or may add a little definition to an image. Locomotive windows can act like mirrors—and locomotives do carry mirrors. These may catch the sun momentarily and a reflection may result in an awkward element in the final image.

In low sun, glint can be effective. Use heavy shadows from buildings, cliff sides or mountains in your composition. Dark shadows can make strong compositional elements.

Elements of the Scene

Is your scene simple or complex? Many effective images feature simple scenes using basic elements. If a scene involves many elements, it can be prioritized so the primary subject has a distinctive emphasis. This can be accomplished in many ways.

The main subject needn't be the largest, most prominent, or even the sharpest photo element. It needs to stand out in some way to direct the eye to it. You may find a scene has too many elements for a single photograph. You may wish to work selectively to produce a stronger single image and leave other elements for separate photographs.

For example, you are photographing a train leaving a busy yard with dozens of tracks and

William D. Middleton

"A lot of patience is required," said William D. Middleton, a transportation and engineering historian who has photographed the railroad scene for more than 50 years.

"Some of the best photographs take advantage of light and weather. Sometimes you just have to wait for the right conditions to get a good photograph."

Middleton—author of 21 books and a contributor to many magazines and trade journals—learned to make pictures to illustrate his writing. He wanted to give magazines a complete package of text and photographs.

His early work was compromised by the lack of good equipment.

"There is no substitute for a sharp lens. Put in enough effort to really learn photography."

A 1950 graduate of Rensselear Polytechnic Institute, he became acquainted with Jim Shaughnessy, then a teenager and the "mascot of the Boomers," a student rail enthusiast group. Shaughnessy went on to pioneer night open flash work. Middleton put Shaughnessy's night work techniques to good use, as well as dramatic panned photographs.

"I was blessed with a natural aptitude for composition, never studied it in any way. It is intuitive. I consciously figure out what a scene is going to look like before clicking the shutter.

"So much of what you see … could have been taken anywhere. I like to step back to get in the landscape, some sense of where the location is. For my favorite photo in Turkey, I drove many miles to get the train in the context with the ruins of Hannibal's castle in the background."

He made his first photos when he was about 10-years-old in the late 1930s in Montana.

"I used a cheap box camera to photograph a Great Northern bridge construction project."

Those negatives are about the only ones he doesn't have now. He has close to 20,000 black and white negatives and thousands of color slides.

"I kept everything. Some of the old bad stuff looks better because it is so rare."

He used an ancient Kodak Autographic, then added an Argus C3 for reliable color slides in the late 1940s and early 1950s. He took some of his best pictures with a 2-1/4" by 3-1/4" Speed Graphic. His first published photos, in *Trains,* were at Monona Tower in Madison in 1949.

Electric interurbans have been an interest since childhood. He had many opportunities to record the interurbans as his family moved across the country. He photographed the Baltimore & Annapolis in the East and Milwaukee Electric Lines in the Midwest.

Finding good spots for photographs always was a form of recreation.

"I got a very good record of the railroad scene wherever I lived during my 29-year Navy career. I have a wonderful photographic record of a variety of places, but it is not all-inclusive."

Middleton likes his black and white photos, especially how they're lighted and printed.

"You are distorting the image you saw in ways that dramatize and emphasize. You can't do that with color. You have a literal record of what is there."

The Railway & Locomotive Historical Society recognized Middleton's work in 1984. He still is taking photographs, although not as actively as he did while serving as co-editor for the monumental Indiana University Press *Encyclopedia of Railroads of North America.* His 50-year record is a tribute to his photographic excellence.

Top: Chicago & North Western 4-6-2 Pacific No. 1550 leads Madison to Chicago train 502 past MX Tower, at Lake Monona, Madison, Wisconsin, on December 24, 1948.

Bottom: The Chicago & North Western train crew on train No. 501, the Chicago to Minneapolis *Viking* compare notes during the station stop at Madison, Wisconsin, on May 16, 1955.

Photos by William D. Middleton

switches. Each switch stand features a lantern with colored signal lights. The main line is protected by an impressive signal bridge with multi-headed signals. On the left is a row of old snow plows. Beyond that is a warehouse with water tanks on top. In the midst of all this is a flock of Canadian geese flying southward over the yard.

One way to make a photograph is to take it all in with a 24mm lens. But you may find all the interesting elements you intended to feature are so small in the photo as to be irrelevant. You failed to convey the scene convincingly. Focus on just a few of elements in a tighter composition.

Framing

One effective compositional technique is framing. By placing a tree, building, or tunnel portal between you and your subject, you can simultaneously add depth, divide your image, and focus your viewer on

The Nenagh Branch train from Ballybrophy to Limerick, approaches the station at Birdhill, Co. Tipperary, in May, 2001. The use of a road overpass as a frame adds depth to a bucolic scene. The image is cross-lit with the sun on the far side of the tracks.

Photo by Brian Solomon
Nikon N90S; 180mm f2.8 Nikkor ED lens; Fuji Sensia (RA) film exposed at f5.6 1/250th

Opposite Page: You never know what may make a photo interesting. This Southern Pacific No. 149, a San Francisco-San Jose "Commute," was exposed at Butler Road in South San Francisco on March 29, 1979. This whole scene has changed. Today all "Commutes" have push-pull sets with locomotives that face away from San Francisco.

Photo by J. D. Schmid
Nikon F2; Kodachrome 25

Mel Patrick

"If you think your pictures are good … only because they have trains in them, there is a problem. If you can't take a picture of something besides a train that somebody wants to see, you have a real problem."

This unusual perspective comes from Denver photographer Mel Patrick, a railroad employee for 34 years. Patrick continually strives for strikingly different images and his pioneering work stretches from synchronized flash to multimedia slide shows.

"The most interesting bit of advice I was ever given was from my fifth grade teacher. I was showing slides at her house in 1971. At the end, she said, 'Are trains all you can photograph?' I needed to broaden my view."

"If you can make an interesting photograph of something besides a train, you are going to make an interesting photograph of something with the railroad in it," says Patrick.

After seeing Winston Link's night photos in *Trains* magazine, he decided to try synchronized flash photography. "I realized then that if you wanted to make an impact, you were going to have to do something unique … there were very few people out there who could do it."

"The trick is to make it look natural, not artificial, and to use the light, in essence, to paint the picture. You are going to highlight those things you want the viewer to see, and let go dark those things that are distracting."

Today, two are continuing the tradition, using equipment he built. "Chris Goepel has a strong eye. Peter Furnée has a newly built version and I've seen his work progress nicely."

Patrick's published work moved from the night photography to the Rio Grande *Zephyr*. He was co-photographer of *Never on Wednesday* (1980), named because the train did not operate on Wednesday.

"As I concentrated on the *Zephyr*, my photography evolved from 'representational' to 'impressionistic'. The trick was to capture the *Zephyr* experience."

Which photographer influenced him? "Easily, everyone! I'm always on the lookout for new ideas, techniques, subjects and locations, never too old or too proud to scarf up a good photo idea."

"Railroads are inherently interesting. A passenger train wasn't simply a passenger train, it was part of a network of postal and express transportation, hotels on wheels for the business traveler, and freight trains built single car service from any shipper to any dock in the U.S. Almost all of that has disappeared."

"The face of railroading had changed, yet the photo opportunities are as exciting as ever. We now have affordable camera equipment and new films that allow us to extend the scope of our vision. I'd like to think that the greatest railroad photo of all time has yet to be taken. The opportunities are ever present. Be there."

M. Ross Valentine watches by moonlight as a Burlington Northern Santa Fe train passes Union Switch & Signal color-lights at East Siberia, California, in March 2000. Mel Patrick said, "This is essence of rail fan photography in the desert—there's the photographer right there!"

This image is about making the best of difficult circumstances. On the flight to California, Patrick's tripod was lost. In order to make due, he placed his F3HP on the ground, removed the prism to adjust the angle, propped the camera with a rock and made this prolonged time exposure.

Photo by Mel Patrick
Nikon F3HP; 16mm Nikkor full-frame fisheye lens; Provia 100F (RDP III) exposed @ f2.8 for about two minutes

the subject or subjects portrayed. Using frames effectively can take careful consideration and practice.

If your foreground frame is too close and your subject too distant, the photograph may be too loosely composed and seem awkward. A properly executed frame may blend subtly with the scene to make the whole image work. Using trees and branches is a favorite tool. They add natural elements to the photograph, but also minimize a bland sky or other obtrusive elements.

A large, graceful tree in the foreground, a colorful train in the middle-ground, and a row of rolling hills gently receding in the background fulfills a conceptual image ideal. A frame such as a window or a hole in trees can completely surround your main subject.

Many frames only partially box in your subject. The side of a building to the left of a train can be used as a visual element that focuses the viewer on a train or railway subject. A frame can be in the background, as well as the foreground. A distant grain elevator, slightly out of focus to one side of the train, can work as a framing element.

Working with a foreground frame, use a wide-angle lens and select a very small aperture for maximum depth of field. It can give relative sharpness to both the frame and the main subject. You can use a longer lens and a wide aperture and allow your

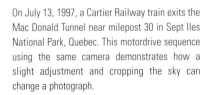

On July 13, 1997, a Cartier Railway train exits the Mac Donald Tunnel near milepost 30 in Sept Iles National Park, Quebec. This motordrive sequence using the same camera demonstrates how a slight adjustment and cropping the sky can change a photograph.

Photos by Brian Solomon
Nikon N90S; 28mm f2.8 Nikkor AF lens;
Fuji Provia (RDP) film

Opposite Page: Just before sunrise on June 9, 1996, a thin mist clings to the Des Moines River Valley, west of Boone, Iowa. A telephoto view of the famous Kate Shelley bridge captures the atmosphere. This composition uses monochromatic light and the bridge's geometry.

Photo by Brian Solomon
Nikon F3T; 200mm f4 Nikkor lens; Fuji Provia 100 (RD) film

A Burlington Northern coal train along the former Northern Pacific line at Beach, North Dakota, on July 12, 1994. Framing for the clouds while exposing for the setting sun creates a stunning silhouette. It's important to keep the horizon below the train's wheels.

Photo by Brian Solomon
Nikon F3T; 35mm PC lens; Kodachrome 25

Burlington Northern Santa Fe freight Q-KCKRIC-1-07 descends the Tehachapi grade between Tunnels 2 and 1 near Caliente, California, on November 7, 1997. Low sun and the broad S-curve accentuate the train in this dramatic landscape.

Photo by Dave Burton
Minolta X700; 50mm lens; Kodachrome 25 @ F4 1/250

frame to be soft and more conceptual. Choose what you feel works more effectively. Experiment with framing and learn how it changes your perception of a scene.

Make a multi-dimensional image. Use frames to split your image and feature two or more subjects in one photo. Make the frame your main subject and alter your photo's emphasis. Focus on your frame, and allow the subject to become abstract. Study the way that famous painters have used frames to produce effective compositions.

A pair of Burlington Northern Santa Fe GE DASH 9-44CWs lead a grain train across the former Northern Pacific bridge over Lake Pend Oreille west of Sand Point, Idaho, on Sept. 9, 1997. This clean composition makes good use of foreground, middle-ground and background elements. The color of the locomotives gives the train nice separation against the distant mountains.

Photo by Tom Kline
Nikon F3; Nikkor 80-200mm f2.8 ED zoom lens; Kodachrome 64 exposed @ f 5.6 1/250

Bridges

Always a favorite subject, bridges have many special considerations. If you photograph a train crossing a large bridge, is your subject the bridge or the train? Do you photograph a bridge from a three-quarter angle, broadside or dead-on?

If you shoot broadside and pull back far enough to take in the whole bridge, your subject—the train—may appear too small. Use a longer lens and focus on the train. Make the train your primary subject and crop the bridge ends. Good execution will make the bridge seem larger. The illusion is caused by the tendency of your imagination to carry the ends of bridge on and on. Every bridge has its own set of visual challenges.

Many deck bridges feature railings that block crucial details of the train as it passes. Depending on the height of the railings, the effect can range from mildly distracting to extremely disruptive to photographic composition.

If the railings are high, you may wish to try shooting down on the bridge to minimize distracting effects of the railings. Alternatively, choose the bridge as your subject and either leave the train out, or allow it to become a minor element in the overall scene. Instead of placing the locomotives close, shoot them in the distance. Use a tripod and make a time exposure of several seconds or more in low light allowing the train to blur across the bridge.

Truss bridges have other considerations. These traditional structures are fascinating compositional elements and are well-suited as subjects. They can be difficult to photograph since a train on a truss bridge can muddle a composition.

If there is space, one solution can be to focus at the end of the bridge and allow the lead locomotive to completely cross the bridge. Feature the train behind the truss. If you can locate a safe vantage point, use a long telephoto and aim down the length of the truss. Frame the locomotives in it at the far end. Or shoot broadside and pan the locomotives as they cross. (See the section on *panning* for technical tips.) You may wish to pan a few of the cars behind the locomotives as well. Moving freight cars in the blur of a truss can be a very effective photograph when it's well executed.

What is the best vantage point to photograph a train on a bridge? If there is a hill or mountain in the distance, behind the bridge, you may wish to try a very low angle view that will put the train crossing the bridge against the sky. This may make a more dramatic picture and will keep a dark train from getting lost in trees and rocks.

If the bridge is crossing water, try getting to water level and use a wide-angle to feature the flowing water in the foreground. This emphasizes the bridge carries the train over water. A bridge also is an excellent venue to make a silhouette. Pick an angle opposite the rising or setting sun and expose for the sky. Open up (lighten) your exposure a little if the sun is beaming through clouds.

For the most dramatic effect, remain broadside of the train. This type of shot can be effective especially when you work with a steam locomotive. Catch the reflection in the water for a bit of symmetry. Make silhouettes of the different types of freight cars.

Tunnels

Tunnels long have been a fascination for artists and photographers alike. It's not easy to make a dramatic photograph of a tunnel. After all, a tunnel is just a big hole. You may try to capture the classic train bursting forth view, or something entirely different. A tunnel portal, tightly framed with the glimmer of a distant headlight, may produce a more compelling image.

The tunnel's darkness draws your eyes to find the distant point of light. Try shooting through a short tunnel, framing the approaching train on the far side. You may need to stand back and use a long telephoto lens.

Try making a sequence of "amazing movie-like images." Find a safe vantage point and keep shooting after the train has entered the tunnel. Get a final photo as the engines enter the light again. You may need several cameras with various focal length lenses or a handy zoom to pull this off effectively.

Often the view from the top of a tunnel is far more impressive than the view of the tunnel portal. If you have limited time, why not make the better shot?

Get the great vista from the top of the tunnel! Try a long time exposure from that viewpoint, using the headlights of an exiting train to illuminate the landscape. Even if the photos don't come out the way you imagined, this is still fun to watch.

Freight trains

North American freight trains are one of the most common topics of contemporary railway photography. Why not show what you are photographing?

Pick a vantage point that will allow you to capture the freight behind the locomotives. Show us what the train is doing! Let us see a heavy train in the mountains running with multiple sets of Distributed Power Units (remote control helpers). Show the gradient, the mountains and the DPUs.

▷

On the evening of June 13, 1990, a Union Pacific eastbound rolls across the Western Pacific's Keddie Wye. To emphasize the bridge, Tom Kline has allowed the train to blur. The yellow dots represent the flashing beacon on top the lead locomotive.

Photo by Tom Kline
Nikon F3; Tamron 28-80mm f2.8 zoom lens, Kodachrome 64 exposed @ f 8 25 seconds

Opposite Page: An empty beet train rolls east of Waterford, along the River Suir, on Iarnród Éireann (Irish Rail), Dec. 8, 2001. The river mirrors the train. A telephoto view from the south bank of the river makes a nicely balanced composition that doesn't include the sky.

Photo by Brian Solomon
Nikon N90S; 180mm f2.8 Nikkor ED lens; Fuji Sensia 100 (RA) film exposed @ f4.5 1/250th

Conrail SD80MACs lead ML482, a loaded auto carrier, east of Palmer, Massachusetts. A 100mm to 400mm zoom at maximum focal length compresses the scene, while framing the train with branches adds depth and drama. Autofocus and image stabilization was used to good advantage.

Photo by Brian Solomon
Canon EOS system Elan; 100-400mm f5.6 Image Stabilization lens; Fuji Astia (RAP) exposed @ f5.6 1/250

On Feb. 21, 1975, an Erie-Lackawanna freight led by SD45-2 3676 and an Alco Century nears West Cameron, New York, along the Canisteo River Valley. This perspective uses over-the-shoulder sun and a three-quarter angle to feature a scenic landscape and an historically interesting train.

Photo by Doug Eisele
50mm lens; Kodachrome film

Christian Goepel

Equally important as the train itself is the anticipation of its arrival. Lighting the way for Chicago Central and Pacific's workhorse train No. 50, the headlight from the leading GP28 backlights the target on the west siding switch at Burlington, Illinois, 53 miles west of the "Windy City" on the former Illinois Central's Iowa Division.

The chirp of crickets and bedroom slumbers soon will be interrupted by a momentary rush of steel-wheeled commerce.

No rule requires a train to be the primary image subject. In this scene, the mainline rail and adjacent siding act as leading lines by converging—directing the viewer past signals, wires, a restored depot, and a grade crossing to the train closing in from infinity.

If you want to show more of the train, you need to pick an appropriate location. Instead of picking a tangent tight to the tracks, find a broad sweeping curve. Put the locomotives on one side of the frame, with the cars spread across the picture. Pick a location with some elevation and shoot across a tight curve. Let us see the entire train trailing behind the far side of the locomotives.

Select a location for a "going away" view. Use a telephoto to compress the train with the locomotives at the far end. Use a long telephoto at relatively low angle to show the grade. This is particularly effective if you select a spot on a curve where the grade changes. A location at the top of a steep grade where the tracks start to level off can be used to show a train "coming up out of a hole." Put the rail in the far corner of the frame and a struggling train off in the distance.

Hard working engines produce heat that can be seen above them as distortion. If they aren't functioning properly and the fuel/air mix is too rich, they will smoke. This can be very impressive. Leave room at the top of the frame to show the smoke.

Do all of this with glint lighting and you have some real drama! An "S-curve" is another good choice to show a train climbing. A little elevation helps. Get back a bit and shoot the S-curve with a medium telephoto. This will give the locomotives and cars a relative size in the photo. Too tight for a horizontal picture? Try a vertical instead.

Opposite Page: Union Pacific coal train crosses a small bridge south of Bill, Wyoming. This image combines panning and silhouette, while making good use of a textured sky at sunset.

Photo by Brian Solomon
Nikon F3T; 28mm f2.8 Nikkor AF lens; Kodachrome 25

Working with Vertical

The previous situation is just one of many where you can select either a vertical or a horizontal format. While it may seem natural to photograph trains in the horizontal format, there are numerous instances where a vertical frame is a better choice. If you have a bit of elevation, such as from a bridge or the top of a tunnel and you select a relatively tight angle, you can make an effective vertical image of the train coming straight on.

A common problem with making vertical images is keeping the framing level. If you've noticed your vertical photos tend to be cockeyed, try using a tripod and line level to keep your camera straight. Carefully watch your horizon. Remember, all you are doing is changing the frame orientation. You don't need to change the position of your head.

Vertical images look great in slide shows, and often are favored by magazine editors for use as cover images and full-page photos.

New SD70MACs shove on a loaded Burlington Northern coal train climbing Nebraska's Crawford Hill on May 29, 1995. This view was made from a hill overlooking a horseshoe curve east of Crawford. The elevated view makes an impressive composition. Clear air and mid-morning sun allow effective use of a long telephoto.

Photo by Brian Solomon
Nikon F3T; 200mm f4 Nikkor lens;
Kodachrome 25 exposed @ f5.6 1/250

Opposite Page: At 5:55 p.m. on Oct. 13, 1985, four Southern Pacific B30-7s and an SD45T-2 lead 01-AVBAK10 (Avondale, Louisiana to Bay Area, California) on the Sunset Route at Benson, Arizona. A long telephoto can show the effects of grade, while pulling in background. The photographer has placed the horizon relatively low in the frame.

Photo by J. D. Schmid
Nikon F2; 300mm f4.5 Nikkor lens;
Kodachrome 25

People

The human element of railway photography is often overlooked. It can be one of the most interesting and rewarding aspects. Some of the most effective railway photos emphasize people. If you find a friendly crew, ask if it's ok to make their photos. Then get in tight, use a wide angle, and show people working. Capture the feeling of working on the railroad. Effective photos often have been made by fellow railroaders. If you work for a railroad, document your coworkers on camera. Or make new friends if you don't work for a railroad.

If you're faced with a cloudy day, make portraits. Soft light is better for portraiture. A short telephoto is useful. Try making an image of an engineer with his engine looming slightly out of focus behind him. Pose a crew in front of their engine. Photographers have been doing this since the dawn of the railroad age.

If it's really dull, use a warming filter—an 81a, b, or c—to give flesh tones a more human color. If it's overcast or harshly lit by a noon sun, fill flash is very helpful.

Working with a Tripod

A tripod is an age-old photographer's tool. Many photographers wouldn't consider setting out in pursuit of images without one. A tripod will keep the camera steady to minimize motion. (The human body has a natural vibration that causes slight blurring in all photographs. Using faster shutter speeds can minimize the blurring, but only separating the camera from the body eliminates it altogether.)

Most railroad photographs exposed at high shutter speeds don't suffer from serious image degradation as a result of camera shake. However, if you're working with long telephoto lenses or making photos in low light, a tripod can greatly reduce blurring and improve the sharpness. Some photographers can hand-hold a telephoto with acceptable sharpness at 1/250th of a second or faster. The speed you can hand-hold a lens and produce acceptable results will depend on many considerations.

You ought to be able to hand-hold a 50mm at speeds as low as 1/60th of second, a 35mm at 1/30th, or a 200mm at 1/250th and so on.

A tripod can be key if you want to maximize your image sharpness. Using a solid tripod is crucial. If your tripod is poorly constructed and conveys vibration or movement through a loose head or a poor materials, it actually can reduce sharpness. A cable release can further minimize the chance for movement.

Fixing a camera in position can greatly improve your composition. Setting your camera on a tripod and adjusting your field of view gives you more opportunity to look at your photograph. This allows you to make fine adjustments in framing, to select the most appropriate focus point, and to make exposure decisions.

A tripod adds discipline to your technique and slows your thought process. Its use requires practice and patience—especially when you're using long telephoto lenses. Tighten all knobs to ensure it won't move suddenly or unexpectedly.

While you're waiting for a train, study your image and ask yourself questions.

- Is the image level? Now is the time to check with your portable line level.
- Have you included enough sky, or too much?
- Do trees or buildings at the frame's edges add or distract from the photograph?
- Look closely for distracting elements.
- Do you need to include a distant poll line? How will this affect the train image?

Engineer Vladimir Krashnikov operates a former Union Pacific General Electric-built C36-7 on Eesti Raudtee (Estonian National Railways). A hand-held Sekonic Studio Deluxe light meter was used to expose for a flesh tone rather than outside conditions.

Photo by Brian Solomon
Contax G2; 28mm f2.8 Zeiss Biogon lens; Fuji Sensia 100 (RA) exposed @ f2.8 1/30

Opposite page: Many accomplished railway photographers are known for their distinctive style. This portrait of Green Bay & Western's Ken Johnson was made when fans were flocking to photograph its aging Alco diesels. It was published in the May 1994 *Trains* magazine.

Photo by John Gruber
Nikon F; 105mm f2.5 lens; Kodachrome 64

Fine adjustments can give your photo better balance and more effective juxtaposition of elements. After close examination, you may find you aren't happy with what you've set up. Move and try a new spot. You don't have to commit a spot to film.

A tripod can free you to work with more than one camera simultaneously. Make a mental note where you want to expose the train. Keep another camera in your hand, perhaps with a different lens and/or film type. Using more than one camera can improve your chances of success, provided you act quickly. Don't let one camera interfere with the other. A tripod can assist you.

How about using two tripods? Set up cameras at different angles—maybe one with a telephoto and another with a wide-angle. Note where you want to expose the train as it passes through each image.

Cold days and steam heat can make for spectacular lighting effects. On Dec. 15, 2001, a steam-heated "Santa train" excursion, run by the Railway Preservation Society of Ireland, pauses at Bray, Co. Wicklow. Exposure was calculated with the camera in matrix meter mode, then adjusted slightly based on experience. Ethereal scenes such as this one last only for a moment, so a photographer needs to anticipate and act quickly.

Photo by Brian Solomon
Nikon N90S; 180mm f2.8 Nikkor ED lens; Fuji Sensia 100 (RA) film exposed @ f8 1/250th

◁ **Opposite Page:** On Good Friday 2000, Gerry Mooney minds Dublin & South Eastern No. 461, a 2-6-0 built in 1923 by Beyer-Peacock in Manchester, England. Afternoon sun fills the cab of the locomotive, which is bathed in its own steam at the Mullingar signal cabin.

Photo by Brian Solomon
Nikon N90S; 105mm f1.8 Nikkor ED lens; Fuji Sensia 100 (RA) film exposed @ f8 1/250th

RAILWAY PHOTOGRAPHY

Tim Doherty

"The first thing to do is to take pictures. Don't accept excuses. You can always find some time," says Tim Doherty, a Massachusetts transit planner.

"Some of my neater pictures have been taken before or after work in early morning or late afternoon light. Often, I get one or two nice pictures in the morning, and in summertime I get off in time for early evening photos."

Practice doesn't always make perfect … but it helps," Doherty continues. "If you want to take really neat pictures, develop your own style."

He took his first railroad pictures in June 1991 at Lackawanna Terminal in Hoboken with his first camera, which wasn't a very good piece of equipment. Fortunately, he says that original camera was stolen and he was able to replace it with better equipment.

He uses about five rolls of film a week throughout the year.

"Film is cheap, your time and gas is not. Film should not be the limiting factor. You want to get the most out of the time as possible. Some days you don't get anything worthwhile, other days you can just clean up."

"Pick one or two good slides from a roll, and focus on trying to improve things. You want publishable quality photos, whether or not you are going to publish them. Whether a rail fan, nature photographer or a photojournalist, you want to get something out of the effort. Shoot with other people. Find people who have different styles. You can learn from their experience. Look at what other rail fans and other photographers are doing. Railroad photography can very easily be clichéd. Have the courage to do something interesting."

He grew up in a family familiar with good photography. That exposure to criticism helped him as he began.

"If you can't make it good, make it big," his father advised, facetiously.

Has everything been done before?

"There are places out there where no one has taken pictures recently. You can go out and do that," he quickly replies.

His example is urban scenes with dramatic skylines.

In New Jersey, he takes pictures in gritty urban areas.

"Playing around with the skyline can make pretty pictures, especially with the tall buildings of Manhattan in the background."

Doherty, who earned a master's degree in urban planning from Rutgers in 1997, says "Skylines with trains are cool. I can do the same thing with a cityscape that others do with a mountain range."

He likes heavy trains and locomotives in the pictures. It has to be an interesting looking train, but doesn't necessarily have to be the most dominant thing in the photographs. He looks for trains in their environment.

"Especially in the East, it's easy to get pictures of trains. What's more important is the bigger, brighter picture. The sense of what is going on and why the train is where it is."

"Challenge yourself," he concludes. "Keep making photographs. If this is something you enjoy doing as you start out, you should be improving exponentially every six months."

Conrail's (TOMT) Toledo to Metuchen, New Jersey, auto parts train at Iona Island on the Hudson River was taken with a Nikon 75-150 3.5 Series E lens, a quality and reasonably priced lens. Look for high quality, inexpensive equipment if you're on a budget.

Photo by Tim Doherty
Nikon N90s; 75-150 f3.5 Nikkor Series E; Fuji Velvia

Preceding Page: West of Cooper, West Virginia, at 8:15 a.m. on Oct. 31, 1987, a Norfolk Southern road power moves "cab-hop" (light engines without train). A telephoto lens, skillful placement of all key elements and subtle use of light have made a distinctive image.

Photo by J. D. Schmid
Nikon F3T; 180 f2.8 ED Nikkor lens; Kodachrome 25 film

Two views from Hitchcock Tunnel on the Seventeen Mile Grade of CSX's Mountain Subdivision in western Maryland. Photos were made about 30 minutes apart in fading evening light. The camera is set on a tripod to maintain consistency between photos and keep the camera steady during long exposures. The photo on top is a one-second exposure at f2.8. The photo below is an eight-minute exposure of a train rolling out of the tunnel and away from the camera.

Photos by Brian Solomon
Nikon F3T; 24mm f2.8 Nikkor lens; Fuji Astia 100 (RAP) film

Opposite Page: Sunset on the Painted Desert in the shadow of the Book Cliffs; a twilight view made along the former Denver & Rio Grande Western at Floy, Utah, on March 1, 1997. Using a wide-angle lens provides a balanced composition, putting elements close and far in relative focus. Would a train improve this photo?

Photo by Brian Solomon
Nikon F3; 28mm f2.8 Nikkor AF lens; Fuji Provia 100 (RDP) film

Some photographers use dual-head tripods. You may be better off mastering one camera before trying to manipulate two or three simultaneously as a train is racing past. Multiple tripod set-ups can be done with practice and discipline.

When action is unfolding quickly, a tripod will prove constraining. If you miss your subject because you were setting up your tripod, you've squandered an opportunity. If setting up a tripod proves difficult, you are better off without one.

Setting up a tripod may attract unwanted attention. Using a tripod may mark you as a "professional" in the eyes of the wrong people and you may find yourself the target of curiosity. Also, it is easier and more effective to pan a train working without a tripod.

◁

Dawn on a clear March 1995 morning at DeKalb, Illinois, depicts Chicago & North Western's massive mainline coal dock. This unused relic of the steam era makes an interesting contrast to modern railroading. Note the location of the horizon.

Photo by Brian Solomon
**Nikon F3T; 135mm f2.8 Nikkor lens;
Fuji Provia 100 (RDP) film**

Opposite Page: Union Pacific SD70M 4370 on the old Los Angeles & Salt Lake Route heading downgrade on Cima Hill on Sept. 21, 2002. A pacing photograph has the similar effect of a pan, but is taken from another vehicle running alongside the train.   ▷

Photo by Tim Doherty
**Nikon N90S; 80-200mm f2.8 Nikkor Zoom lens;
Provia 100F**

In July 1963, a South Shore interurban train stops for passengers on the streets of Michigan City, Indiana. Rather than make a conventional three-quarter view, Richard Jay Solomon chose an angle that conveyed the spirit of the scene.

Photo by Richard Jay Solomon
Leica M3, 50mm f2 Summicron lens;
Kodachrome II (ASA 25)

Pan Shots

An effective way of capturing the motion of the railway is by panning a train as it passes. Properly executed, a pan will leave the train in sharp focus, while blurring the foreground and background. The effect shows a train racing across the landscape.

Follow the train with your camera and expose at a relatively slow shutter speed. By keeping train and frame movements even, the train will remain sharp while everything else blurs. This can be accomplished with a variety of different lenses, but one of the best is a short telephoto (85 to 105mm) on a 35mm camera.

It can be difficult to execute an effective pan with a long telephoto because you need to use a slow shutter speed, and the lens may cause excessive vertical blurring. The unwanted body motion will cause the entire photo to appear blurry. A wide-angle lens (especially a super-wide) also can pan a train because a narrower vertical plane remains completely sharp as the camera moves. A "normal" lens (50mm in 35mm film format) is another good tool for making pan photographs.

The train's speed, the shutter speed you select, and the angle all affect the pan. If a train is moving at a nominal speed, say 30 to 50 mph, shoot broadside at 1/30th of a second. The pan will convey considerable motion, but won't make the background unrecognizable.

Blurring will become more pronounced as you lower the speed, but it becomes more difficult to keep the train sharp. A 1/60th or 1/125th may result in just a slightly blurred background, yet is enough to convey motion.

Panning is most effective if you turn your entire body to follow the train's movement, not just your head and upper body. A smoother, more consistent body motion when panning will make the train appear sharper. This takes a bit of practice.

You may wish to practice panning cars on a fast-moving freeway before making your first railway pans. Keep the nose of the locomotive at the same place in the frame as you pan. Avoid over-panning (moving the camera too fast) or under-panning (moving too slowly).

Follow through with your panning motion and don't stop the instant you release the shutter. This a common problem with inexperienced pan photographers who jerk to a stop at the moment they press the shutter button and lose the effect of a smooth, unbroken pan. When you have set up at your location, make several practice pans before the train arrives.

If you're working with low depth of field (a large lens aperture opening) and a manual focus camera, it may be best to pre-focus on the place where you expect to release the shutter. It can be very difficult to focus and pan simultaneously. Also, you will want to preset your exposure. If you're working with a camera that features automatic exposure and autofocus capabilities, this may be a good time to let the camera make decisions so you can concentrate on a smooth, even pan. If you have a motor drive, keep shooting as you pan. You can go through a bit of film this way, but may produce spectacular results. If you don't have a motor drive or winder, carefully plan the moment of your shutter release.

A Yamanote Loop train near Ueno Station in Tokyo on April 21, 1997. The train is one element in a complex, layered, urban scene. Soft lighting has been used positively. Stronger light could simplify the scene by minimizing the foreground or background.

Photo by Brian Solomon
Nikon N90S; 28mm f2.8 Nikkor lens; Fuji Provia 100 (RDP) film exposed @ f4.5 1/250th

Panning is an excellent technique for conveying speed and motion. Panning successfully takes patience and sometimes a bit of practice. In July 2002, a VR (Finnish State Railways) Sr-2 electric accelerates past the yard at Oulu with an express passenger train bound for Helsinki. A rangefinder camera with a smooth shutter release makes sharp pans easier.

Photo by Brian Solomon
Contax G2; 28mm f2.8 Zeiss Biogon lens; Fuji Sensia 100 (RA) exposed @ f22 1/30

◁ **Opposite Page:** John Conn worked at the Boston & Albany shops in West Springfield, Massachusetts. Later, he helped save the B&A's Ware River Branch from abandonment and helped create the Mass-Central. John faces a brisk morning at Ware, Massachusetts, in 1987.

Photo by Brian Solomon
Rolleiflex T; with f3.5 Zeiss Tessar; exposed with 645 insert for rectangular format

▷

On Nov. 1, 1985, Conrail workmen align a new limited-speed turnout at Palmer, Massachusetts. Conrail converted the old Boston & Albany from traditional, directional, double-track to a modern single-track route directed by Centralized Traffic Control.

Photo by Brian Solomon
Rolleiflex T; with f3.5 Zeiss Tessar; exposed with 645 insert for rectangular format; Kodak Verichrome Pan rated at 80 ASA

Panning is a useful technique for solving visual problems. It can be used to simplify the appearance of a complex and distracting background. And it can separate a train from the background. If you're faced with black or dark-colored locomotives against a background of poorly lit evergreen trees, try panning.

Panning also can make a dramatic photograph on a dull day. If you face low light and contrast in an interesting place, pan and keep the scene interesting. If it's a very bright day with harsh overhead sun, a pan will help reduce the contrast between your subject and the background.

Experiment by shooting through trees with gaps in them. Allow the trees to blur. Two freight trains passing across a field from you? Pan one train and let the other blur. Interested in making photos of freight cars? Pan them broadside crossing a bridge. Pan interesting or colorful graffiti on a box car as it rolls by. Try panning trains against varieties of backgrounds—mountain landscapes, industrial cityscapes, farms, or even a busy station platform.

A variation is the *pacing photo*. This requires another vehicle or another train that is moving at the same speed and is parallel to the train you wish to photograph. Ideally, you either want to be even with the front of the train or slightly ahead of it, looking back.

If you are doing this with a car, have a driver who understands what is required help you. We don't recommend trying this alone! Plan your strategy and discuss it with your driver. Find a stretch of highway that parallels the tracks. Drive along with the train. If it is moving fast, get some speed before the train is on you. It's best to do this on a lightly traveled road. Motorists cannot be expected to understand what you are doing.

Pull ahead of the train and shoot back at it, varying your shutter speed. With pan photos, 1/60th of a second often works well. Photos with slower shutter speeds are likely to suffer from vertical road vibrations that can cause undesirable image degradation. Avoid bushes, trees, and poles that pass in front of you. If you're not careful, you may find that every time you release the shutter, a pole intersects the locomotive. Watch your foreground, too. You are best to execute pacing photos from the passenger side of the car to avoid including the road. Some camera manufacturers, such as Canon, offer image stabilizer lenses. These can produce excellent results with pacing and panning.

CHAPTER 5

LOCATION, LIGHT, LENSES

◀

Opposite Page: Southern Pacific's BKDOL (Bakersfield to Dolores, California—unit oil train) climbs toward Tehachapi in Feb. 1991. This train was among the heaviest operated by SP at that time, weighing as much as 13,500 tons, and operated with a mid-train helper cut-in about two-thirds deep. The use of a 200mm lens accentuates the effect of the Tehachapi grade, while the low sun increases the drama by back-lighting the exhaust from the locomotives. Minutes after this image was exposed, the sun set behind the mountains.

Photo by Brian Solomon
Nikon F3T; 200mm f4 Nikkor lens; Kodachrome 25

✳ **Location**

Choosing the location is one of the most important decisions in making railway photographs. Location is a crucial element of a successful image, and can be its central focus. In many great historic photographs location is *the* subject, while individual railway elements are incidental. When we see a good photo of the Horseshoe Curve, Tehachapi Loop, or London's Paddington Station, the trains are secondary. In a photograph of a shiny new locomotive, the location is almost irrelevant.

Photographers choose locations for proximity, familiarity, accessibility, scenic virtue, quality of light, weather, and intensity of operation. A location that is close to where you live and easily reached by car or on foot has advantages because you can get there quickly and often.

Yet they may have infrequent railway activity, an ugly setting or undesirable angles. While you may visit a close, easy spot often, it may not be the best place to devote your photographic efforts.

The most popular spots in the American West are internationally known for their ease of access, spectacular scenery, fantastic weather, and heavy action. Locations in Tehachapis, Cajon Pass, the old Santa Fe mainline across the Mojave Desert and Arizona, are featured repeatedly in magazines and books. They fulfill the ideals associated with traditional railway photography.

Unless you live near these places, getting there regularly is difficult. Because so much photography is done at these places, the angles and trains may seem trite or clichéd.

Working Locally

Selecting locations will depend on your time. If you only have a few hours, you will be limited to locations close to home. If you have several weeks, you will have nearly infinite choices.

The ultimate quality of your photographs ought not be dependant on distance. It's a mistake to believe the best photos are taken a great distance from home. Plan a strategy to work around your time. Locations close by are advantageous. Make the best use of repeated visits. If you live near a railway, take time daily to gather information and visual reconnaissance.

Study day-to-day operating patterns like when trains run and which trains may be the most interesting to photograph. Perhaps a freight that serves local industries regularly runs with older locomotives that soon will be sold or scrapped. If these

Opposite Page: Southern Pacific's Coast Line near Jalama Beach, California. A wide angle lens captured the Pacific Ocean's expanse, while allowing the side of the train to be lit by the sun. Elevation puts the train in better light, giving the perspective needed to show the Pacific and the beach. A lower angle may not have worked as effectively.

Photo by Brian Solomon
Nikon F3T; 28mm AF Nikkor lens;
Kodachrome 25 exposed @ f4 1/500

On Oct. 14, 1993, Central Vermont 323 departed the yard at Brattleboro, Vermont, before dawn. By following through the Connecticut River Valley, it was possible to select a vantage point that best captured the morning sun. This spot on the New Hampshire side of the Connecticut River (opposite Windsor, Vermont) had been scoped out in advance. By driving several minutes ahead of the train there was time to set up a tripod and make a light reading with a hand-held Sekonic Studio Deluxe light meter. Mt. Ascutney looms in the distance.

Photo by Brian Solomon
Nikon F3T; 200mm f4 Nikkor lens;
Kodachrome 25

An overcast scene at Tunnel Hill in Gallitzin, Pennsylvania, was briefly pierced by a window of sun in May 2002 just as a Norfolk Southern train crawls toward the summit of the Alleghenies. Recognizing a fortuitous moment and acting quickly is important. The light falling in this way directs the viewers eye toward the train and accents it.

Photo by Brian Solomon
Nikon N90S; 180mm f2.8 Nikkor lens;
Fuji Astia exposed @ f5.6 1/320

A location demonstrating cosmic lighting effects on one occasion may obtain similar effects under the right conditions. These shots were made at the 'Railfan's Bridge' over the Boston & Maine yard at East Deerfield, Massachusetts, over a 13-year span.

The first photo (at top) was made in September 1989 as thick fog burned off the Connecticut River. The second (at bottom) was made in October 2001 shortly after sunrise when a light mist filled the yard. The third (opposite page) made in October 2002 in heavy fog.

Photos by Brian Solomon

locomotives interest you, their proximity can allow you to find the best locations to capture them.

You can become accustomed to the switching patterns. Learn the traffic the train carries, and better relate this train to its environment. If it carries a single commodity, like cement, potash, coal, copper or timber, show how this traffic relates to the community.

Include some related industries in a photograph. Even if the operation is infrequent, you may have a better chance of photographing a line nearby than traveling hundreds of miles. Make the most of local railway lines.

While you may have only a little time for excursions, the amount of time studying and photographing adds up. Your repeated trips can help you explore different angles, hone your skills, and perfect your technique.

Your back yard may not be one of the great mountain passes of the American West, but you still can take great photos there. Avoid developing contempt for familiar places. Use familiarity to make the best possible photographs. A dull location at midday may be a fantastic place to photograph in the early morning or at night.

Observation may help you find a great photographic opportunity from an unusual vantage point. This may require a long walk to the top of a

hill. Perhaps an owner's permission is required to access private property. Befriend the owner and obtain permission to return when the light is right and the train is running. Be sure to offer the property owner a copy of a nice shot. A free print or two can go a long way.

More familiarity with operations will help you recognize the unusual. Has the local early morning freight been delayed? Is there a perfect westbound location that would look nice for an unusual afternoon move?

Finding Locations

Have patience and use all the resources available to you to find good locations.

Maps are a very good way to find potential locations. You never really know if a place on the map is a good location until you inspect it. A more detailed, accurate map will help. Use maps that show railway lines as well as roads.

The U.S. Geological Survey maps are an excellent resource. Exceptionally detailed, they use topographical lines to convey elevation. They indicate bodies of water, major structures, infrastructure and natural landmarks. USGS maps help you trace railway lines and find good photo locations. The most detailed USGS maps are the best.

Complete sets of USGS maps can be found at major public city and university libraries. Photocopy the sections that cover the railway and assemble them in geographical order. Put them in a binder. Using photocopies allows you to make notes without marking up original maps.

Some older USGS maps may show abandoned railways. This information is beneficial to help you track the heritage of different lines—especially useful if several companies once operated in an area. Acquiring a large number of detailed USGS maps is costly and they can be awkward to handle on location. Companies like DeLorme and National Geographic sell USGS style maps on CD Rom.

In recent years, DeLorme has produced a series of atlas and gazetteer map books for many states. While not as detailed as USGS maps, they're a great resource for following the tracks and finding locations.

In Great Britain and Ireland, ordinance survey maps show great detail and are valuable tools. The Global Positioning System (GPS) may also be useful.

Use maps to locate bridges, tunnels, cuts, and fills. Even a bridge over a small creek may present a great spot. Even a few feet of elevation is better than track level. Watch for places where elevation is outside of a curve, or better, is in the middle of an S-curve or horseshoe curve.

Trace the route of a railway line on your map. Often, when a line pulls away from main roads, ducks into a river valley, or climbs over a mountain pass, scenery is at its most spectacular, although access can become more difficult. Keep this in mind when you're looking for shots along the highway.

⊳

On the morning of July 14, 1991, an eastward Southern Pacific train doubled the hill between Midas and Emigrant Gap on the ascent of Donner Pass. Recoupling of its train allowed for some static photos of this Cotton Belt GP60. This image was made using a 35mm perspective control lens to keep the vertical lines straight and a circular polarizing filter to minimize the effects of harsh summer light by reducing sun glare from tree branches.

Photo by Brian Solomon
Nikon F3T; 35mm PC Nikkor lens;
Kodachrome 25

⊲ **Opposite Page:** Is there interesting equipment in a tight spot? Try a fisheye lens and do something wild. A pair of derelict Electro-Motive F-units along the old Rock Island at Limon, Colorado, made an interesting composition with a 16mm full-frame fisheye.

Photo by Brian Solomon
Nikon F3T; 16mm Nikkor full-frame fisheye
lens; Fuji Provia 100 (RDP)

Sometimes a combination of light, preparedness and serendipity can form a remarkable image. M. Ross Valentine was photographing at the Ji-Tong Railway's steam locomotive maintenance facility at Daban, Inner Mongolia, China, on Feb. 19, 2003.

"I was walking around searching for 'glint' light," says Valentine. "I noticed one of the workers with a shovel … silhouetted against the sky. Suddenly, the movement of his shoveling coal stirred up enough dust to form a cloud between us. It created a unique shadow between the camera, his silhouette, and the evening light. This moment lasted only a few seconds, enough time to make only one photo. It was gone in an instant."

Photo by M. Ross Valentine
Canon EOS 3; Canon 70-200 f2.8 "L" Image stabilized lens; Fujichrome Provia 400F

When photographing people, knowing their personality, body language—and even their misgivings—are all crucial for them to appear as they are in real life. Engineer Travis Berryman waits in the siding at Halls Flat, California, on July 7, 1999. Despite the mundane locomotive cab, a routine event can define a sense of time and place.

Photo by M. Ross Valentine
**Nikon N-70; 28mm f2.8 lens;
Agfa Scala 200x—shot at ASA 200**

M. Ross Valentine

"Follow your bliss. Do what makes you happy. Do the things you feel strongly about. Take pictures that satisfy yourself, not others. Photography should be a spiritually satisfying journey."

These words come from Detroit photographer M. Ross Valentine who has traveled from the desert West to Europe and China in his search for new and creative views.

It has been absolutely satisfying for him.

"I wound up doing things I wouldn't have done ordinarily. Certainly, I wouldn't have been on a steam locomotive running at 100 mph in Austria, or got frost bite above my eye where I held my camera in a wind chill of 53 degrees below zero in Inner Mongolia."

A trip on the railroad car ferry across Lake Michigan with his grandparents hooked him. Later, a friend at a hobby shop introduced him to railroad photography. Until then, he wasn't aware that people took train pictures. He purchased his first 35mm camera in 1984.

He is familiar with overseas travel, since he was married in Austria in 1992 and lived there for five years. He studied at the University of Innsbruck from 1993 to 1997, when he and his wife, Agnes, left for the U.S.

"Overseas you get a feeling of freedom not found here. A place has newness. You can represent it photographically any way you like. You have no notion of how a place should be before you go there. Essentially you have a blank canvas. You learn about yourself and your own country. It's very positive experience."

"Many foreign railroads don't have to deal with liability issues. They are more willing to let you in cabs of locomotives and towers and depots. … overseas you have the ability to photograph things that haven't been a part of the railroad scene here for two to three decades: Small rural country stations, semaphores, and passenger trains."

Valentine suggests starting in countries similar to our culture, such as Western Europe.

"Luckily, English ends up as the common language of the world. Sometimes you will be forced to communicate in ways you wouldn't think of. … fear of the language is something you quickly overcome."

For Valentine, two weeks in China in February 2003 was outstanding. Traveling to Inner Mongolia, he and a friend hired guides to see steam locomotives in the winter. He will go back as soon as he gets the opportunity.

The human aspect of railroading fascinates him. "An equipment photo with a person in it instantly becomes alive. The easiest way to express emotion is to have somebody in it. To be good at it, you have to establish trust with your subjects, so you can see their real personality."

He has written articles for *Trains*, *CTC Board*, and his pictures have appeared in European publications. He received a grant from the Austrian Federal Railway and the Tyrolean Ministry for Arts and Culture for a project on the railroads of Tyrol.

He has given slide programs in Italy, Switzerland, and Austria.

He admires the color work of Galen Rowell, and recommends *Galen Rowell's Vision*, *The Art of Adventure Photography* (1993). Sebastiao Salgado and David Plowden also influenced him.

Valentine repeats words from Rowell he found helpful: "People avoid developing a personal style by emotionally distancing themselves from their work. They make images filled with information instead of emotion."

Valentine says: "If you have a true passion, it will transcend though your photos."

Above: For a moment on July 6, 1994, the clouds parted and afternoon sun rays were shining on the Rocky Mountains east of Glacier National Park, Montana. Exposing for the sky and allowing the shadow areas to go dark captured this moment on film. Had the camera been set to expose the tracks, the effect of the sun may have been lost.

Photo by Brian Solomon
Nikon F3T; 105mm f1.8 Nikkor lens; Kodachrome 25

As the tracks leave the road, your best opportunities may be at hand.

Railroad employee timetables, track diagrams, and grade profiles are helpful. A timetable will reveal passing sidings, junctions, and significant infrastructures, including detailed milepost indications. Track profiles present information in schematic graphics.

Grade profiles can determine the steepest tracks. A steep grade has advantages. Trains working harder increase drama. They don't move as fast, making photography easier. A telephoto lens can compress the effects of the grade, making it look impressive. The bottom of a climb and the top of a grade can be the best places to witness the effects of the grade.

Timetables and maps can help you better understand a railroad and learn how it relates to places it serves. Perhaps a spur once served an old mine. Maybe the line was relocated after a flood and the old right of way runs parallel to it. This information can help you make more interesting photographs.

Instead of just getting a shot of a train rolling through the woods, compose a juxtaposition of the old line with the new. Use a train as a story component with one image, or perhaps using a sequence of shots.

The wealth of railway publications available today can assist you in finding good potential locations. Many magazines published in the U.S.—*CTC Board Railroads Illustrated*, *Train Magazine*, *Railpace*, and *Railfan & Railroad*—print detailed articles on different lines.

In Europe, *Today's Railways* occasionally publishes descriptions of photogenic lines. Magazine articles often are accompanied by maps designed to assist railway photographers, though detail and usefulness varies greatly.

Finding the specific back issue about an area you wish to photograph can be a quest for the Holy Grail. Back issues sometimes can be found in libraries. You can contact railway magazine publishers for recent issues, but most publishers usually keep only some of their most recent issues on hand. After a few months or years, back issues usually aren't for sale.

Railroad expositions, model train shows, antique shops, and used book stores can be good sources. And the Internet can be another good source for back issues. Other photographers are some of the best sources for location information. Make friends and share your knowledge of local places and useful techniques. Commercial railroad videos can also be used by the clever photographer to spot potential locations. Again, the Internet is a powerful tool for researching locations. Railroad employee timetables, passenger schedules, and freight symbols are all available on the Internet. If you are interested in photographing a suburban passenger operation, check that agency's Web page for

scheduling.

Railroad employee timetables, passenger schedules and freight symbols all are available on the Internet. If you're interested in photographing a suburban passenger operation, check that agency's Web page for scheduling.

Time and Light

Naturally, one factor leads to discussing the other. Optimize your time and plan to put yourself in position for the very best photographs.

Morning

The day dawns clear and bright, a clear blue dome prevails overhead as the first rays of sun gently burn mist off the stream and fields. Unless you're already on location, you've squandered the best light of the day.

We have many excuses for ignoring morning, but excuses can't change the reality of rich morning light. To take advantage of it, you have to be there—not lying in bed or on the road to your spot. The next best thing to a bright morning is a sunny afternoon. Just because the morning was clear, doesn't mean hazy clouds won't ruin the afternoon. Use the light when you have it.

Plan and be flexible. Study local weather patterns. Know when the sun rises, and have your morning locations staked out in advance. Make the most of a good day with an early start. Rise well before sunrise so you can get where you need to be by daybreak. If you know a railroad's traffic patterns, you can be where a train catches the first rays of morning sun.

Tightly scheduled runs, such as passenger and intermodal trains, can be your best bets. Putting the train together with the light takes patience. You may go out again and again just to get the right shot. Over time, this can pay off with spectacular results.

If the railroad follows a road, another strategy is to follow the train into the light. This may require one or more dry runs to work out highway timing versus railroad timing. Pick up a train before dawn, follow it, and get ahead of it at sunrise to make your photos. If this is a regular run, you may be able to do this repeatedly and hone your technique.

Predicting Weather

America's National Weather Service, local and national television, radio, and newspapers all provide weather information. Other good sources for weather news are the Weather Channel, and Web-based Internet sites. (See the resources in the back of

this book.) It's now possible to check radar maps and satellite images from a laptop computer connected to a mobile phone.

The weather savvy railway photographer may have an advantage over the more casual weather observer. As good as modern weather forecasting is, there are potential problems. Forecasting is only someone's best guess. Weather is extraordinarily complicated and affected by many variables, so forecasts aren't always accurate.

For example, you are peering into the pre-dawn gloom, doubting the forecast of morning sun and listening to pouring rain. You decide to sleep in. What if the pre-dawn rain ends and a beautiful, clear day prevails? If you're not trackside, it's too bad for you.

Ordinary weather forecasts aren't tailored to the needs of railway photographers. Forecasts may be useful for planning your morning work commute or planning a picnic, but are not sufficiently

Opposite Page: It's challenging to capture what the eye sees on film. Falling snow doesn't necessarily photograph well. A telephoto can compress the snow effect, making it appear more prominent. This scene was made on St. Patrick's Day 1991. A Southern Pacific unit coal train descends Donner Pass at Yuba Pass, California.

Photo by Brian Solomon
Nikon F3T; 200mm f4 Nikkor lens; Kodachrome 25 exposed @ f4+ 1/3 stop at 1/250

High sun is extremely contrasty, yet it can be used to make interesting photos. When working in high light, use elevation and shoot down on a subject. The angle and lighting are used to feature some of the locomotive's distinguishing characteristics: A large front platform and SP's trademark headlight arrangement.

Photo by Brian Solomon
Nikon F3T; 105mm f1.8 Nikkor lens; Kodachrome 25

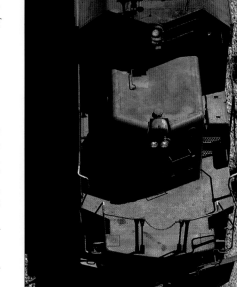

accurate to decide when to make photographs. "Partly sunny" often means a thin veil of cloudiness that may not provide good light for photos.

And general weather forecasts tend to cover a fairly wide area. Where micro-climates present locally diverse weather, a general forecast may be irrelevant. During summer in the Appalachian Mountains, a dense morning fog forms in river valleys. Despite a sunny forecast, you may find your location is socked in. It is sunny, just not where you are. Local weather knowledge may be more helpful in these situations.

◁

Opposite Page: At 7:04 p.m. on Oct. 14, 1985, Southern Pacific B30-7s lead the WCKCM (West Colton, California, to Kansas City) past vintage Union Switch & Signal semaphores at Vail, Arizona. The exhaust smoke signals the locomotives are working hard.

Photo by J. D. Schmid
Nikon F2; 180mm f2.8 ED Nikkor lens; Kodachrome 25 exposed @ f2.8 1/60

At Right: Western Pacific WPX climbs through the Feather River Canyon west of Belden, California, on Nov. 11, 1979. Metallic surfaces of railway equipment reflect back-lit sun. Keep the sun from hitting the front element of the lens, reducing flare. Expose for glint manually. A camera meter may compensate for the darkness and overexpose the shot. ▷

Photo by J. D. Schmid
Nikon F2; Kodachrome 25

Understanding local weather patterns can help you better interpret the forecast and plan when and where you will set up. In that deep river valley, there may be a place where the sun hits first on the valley floor or you may have seen the sun slice a hole in the fog, creating cosmic effects. Such weather effects often are repeatable.

Large bodies of water—lakes, oceans, and rivers—all affect local weather patterns. So do hills and mountains. This may seem obvious, but at the specific level, it may be more difficult to determine how the weather will be affected. Often it may rain on one side of a mountain range while sun shines on the other. It may be cloudy along the coast, but clear a few miles inland. A valley may be basking in sunlight, while the hilltops are lost in the clouds. All this may happen while the general forecast shows sunshine.

A few miles west of Chester, Massachusetts, on CSX's Boston Line, a train negotiates a sharp curve in a rock cutting between mileposts 128 and 129. The railroad crosses the West Branch of the Westfield River twice in a short distance, in a narrow, foggy valley. A gap in the hillside provides a window for the rising sun. It results in the sun burning off fog here first. The lighting effects can be stunning. The fog effects usually are best in late summer and early autumn.

Other places like this include Mill Creek, Pennsylvania, along the old Pennsylvania Railroad mainline (now operated by Norfolk Southern). It's accessible by State Highway 22, which runs parallel to the railroad. The east end of CSX's old Baltimore & Ohio yard at East Grafton, West Virginia, is another example. In winter, this effect can be seen near Boca Dam in the Truckee River Canyon on the former Southern Pacific crossing of Donner Pass.

The wonderful thing about morning light is its changeability. This tumultuous time, when night dissolves into day, often has cosmic weather effects. The weather can be good or bad, but sometimes you are best to persevere regardless of present conditions.

This might be the morning the forecasters hit it right, so you get to your "known good spot" just in time to catch the sun bursting from the storm clouds as the first eastbound freight rolls into view.

Some photographers call this "drop under" when the sun illuminates clouds from below causing spectacular effects. Add a bit of fog and rain and you can get a cosmic image. You cannot make that shot if you wait in bed for the weather to improve.

Low Sun vs. High Sun

All things being equal, the quality of light is better when the sun is low. The tonality is warmer, the light is richer and softer, and low light angles allow more versatile, creative approaches to photography.

If the morning isn't for you, the weather is spotty, or any number of other excuses prevent you from taking advantage of morning light, the afternoon and evening are the next best time. Low sun and the prospect of interesting weather effects can make evening nearly as rewarding as morning. (And you get more sleep!)

What's wrong with shooting in high sun? High sun is harsh, contrasty, unflattering light that generally doesn't photograph well. From a technical perspective, greater exposure difference increases contrast. High, polarized sun makes highlights brighter and shadows darker. On clear days, higher amounts of blue light accentuate contrast. Films such as Kodachrome tend to be less sensitive to the blue spectrum, making blue appear darker than other colors. That makes the situation worse.

"High sun" is at its worst in the middle of the day, especially in the summer. The effect of blue light is severe at high elevations, such as the California Sierra, Colorado Rockies, or Swiss Alps. And the closer you are to the equator, the longer the period of undesirable high sun. Generally, the light is harsher.

◁

Photographer Pete Ruesch says: "The moral behind this shot is, 'watch the sky and use your head.' I was living about 12 miles from the location of this semaphore on the old Monon (now CSX). A slow-moving thunderstorm was working its way east. I looked west and could see a golden glow … clear sky in that direction. Surprisingly, things fell into place. A train was approaching as I took the photo, but the sun and the rainbow were gone by the time it reached me."

Photo by Pete Ruesch
Canon EOS 100; Fuji Velvia

Opposite Page: Strong, low light can focus ▷ attention on select subjects in a complex scene. Choose your vantage point to make the most effective use of light. This photograph of a PCC on Pittsburgh streets was made in 1963. Note the various Pennsylvania icons in the image.

Photo by Richard Jay Solomon
Leica M3; 50mm f2 Summicron lens;
Kodachrome film

Opposite Page: Photographers George S. Pitarys and Brian Solomon spent several days in January 1998 photographing Iron Road Railways' Quebec Southern. This exposure was made at Cookshire, Quebec, at sunrise. The clouds that made for the rosy morning glow would soon prevail, leaving a flat gray day. Get up early and photograph!

Photo by Brian Solomon
Nikon N90S; Fuji Provia 100 (RDP)

One of the best times to work with artificial light is when there still is a hint of daylight. This makes a more even exposure, lowers contrast, and reduces the time needed to make the photo, while adding a bit of color. A streetcar pauses on Baltimore Avenue in Philadelphia in November 1997.

Photo by Brian Solomon
**Nikon N90S; 24mm f2.8 AI lens;
Fuji Provia 100 (RDP)**

A CSX coal train led by modern GE-built AC4400CWs descends through Moss Run, Virginia, on March 7, 2002. Photographers seeking a high degree of sharpness can work with fine grain films such as Fuji's Provia F (RDP III). The manufacturer rates it as having a diffuse RMS granularity rating of 8, one the sharpest films on the market.

Photo by T. S. Hoover
**Nikon F3HP; 55mm f2.8 Nikkor lens;
Fuji Provia 100F (RDPIII) exposed @ f4 1/1000**

Opposite Page: In July 2002, a Green Cargo Rc4 electric emerges from a snow shed on the line to Narvik, Norway, north of the Arctic Circle. An image featuring a relatively small train in a spectacular setting can be effective. The eye quickly is drawn to the green electric.

Photo by Brian Solomon
**Contax G2; 28mm f2.8 Biogon lens;
Fuji Sensia 100 (RA) exposed @ f8-11 1/250**

California's Tehachapis are a favorite venue for railway photographers. In some situations the bucolic scenery is more compelling than the railroad. This image, looking toward Tunnel One, features a Southern Pacific train in a less prominent role, giving the splendor of the mountains the glory they deserve.

Photo by Brian Solomon
**Nikon F3T; 35mm PC Nikkor lens;
Kodachrome 25 exposed @ f8 1/60**

On the flip side, high sun is less severe the further north you go. In northerly locations, harsh midday light merely is a nominal concern. In Arctic regions, high sun isn't a problem, even in mid-summer.

Many photographers choose to avoid shooting in high sun. In the continental United States, a general guideline for avoiding the effects of high sun means refraining from color photography between 10 a.m. and about 3 p.m. from the end of April until the end of August. Generally, your time would be better spent engaging in photo reconnaissance and planning, eating lunch, traveling, or visiting with friends.

Coping with Midday

If the specific train you want to photograph runs only at noon, make photos at a time of year when high sun is less of a problem. If possible, move two or three hours down the line. If this isn't possible, choose a location that will minimize the undesirable effects of high sun. If you must work at noon in mid-June (perish the thought!), avoid backlighting. This is not the time to look for a 'glint shot.' Even slightly backlit shots can be very harsh. A wide angle lens may be a better choice than a telephoto.

Choose a location with good elevation so you can look down. Use a low contrast film. We've found Fuji's Sensia 100 is one of the best choices in high sun. Traditional Kodachrome films are among the worst because they tend to exaggerate harsh lighting.

Perhaps your best bets are traditional black and white films, providing you do your own processing. Adjusting your exposure, developer, and processing times during film processing can significantly lower contrast.

Option 1: Use Kodak Tri-X, rated at 200 ISO, and process it in plastic tanks. Use Ilfotec HC developer (mixed one part developer to 32 parts water) at 70 degrees F for three minutes, 45 seconds, agitating with three gentle inversions every minute. Agitate

again just before emptying the developer. Stop, fix, hypoclear, and wash as normal. If you are shooting 120/220 film, use a four-minute developing time.

By following this formula, you are increasing the amount of detail in the shadows that is suffering from underexposure while giving the highlights less processing time. This reduces both the highlight density and the contrast of your negatives. Assuming everything else is constant, including the film speed rating, this is about a 7 percent reduction in processing time from that used for film exposed in normal lighting.

Option 2: Using your normal developer, cut processing time by 7 to 15 percent and see what the result is like. Before risking an untried formula on critical film, experiment on a test role that isn't crucial to you.

Afternoons

A bright sunny afternoon is a great time to make photos. You will enjoy most of the benefits of morning sun, without having to rise before the sun.

➤

In a scene that looks like it was taken from a 1960s thriller, we look into the gloom of night on the Burlington Northern Santa Fe. The scene is pierced by red lights from signals at Mendota, Illinois.

Photo by Steve Smedley
F5; 300mm f4.5 AI Nikkor; Professional Kodachrome 64 (PKR); f5.6 @ 9 seconds

◁ **Opposite Page:** Sometimes the most effective photos can be made in the driving rain. In October 2000, a Guilford freight led by Canadian Pacific SD40-2 5640 rolls through Charlemont, Massachusetts, toward the Hoosac Tunnel on the old Boston & Maine Fitchburg Route.

Photo by Brian Solomon
Nikon N90S; 180mm f2.8 ED Nikkor lens; Fuji Astia 100 (RAP)

It's All About Atmosphere   by Howard Ande

Like most photographers, I enjoy shooting on clear, sunny days when colors jump out against a blue sky. However, I would almost always opt for what I call "atmosphere." I'd describe this as fog, mist, blowing snow, or rays of sun as a subtle source of mood in a darkened scene.

Atmosphere is fleeting, fickle, and usually occurs at dawn or dusk when day mixes with night. It doesn't last long. The morning sun rises too high. In the evening, it sets and is gone. Usually early morning is a good bet for working with misty, foggy, or muted lighting. When the sun starts to burn dew or fog, dramatic lighting occurs.

The beauty of photographing the railroad in atmospheric lighting is the subtle soft rays reflecting off the hard angular lines of track, railroad infrastructure, and trains. I've found I liked a railroad scene best without a train—when the subtle light of late day mixes with weather phenomenon.

The morning sun burns off the fog at St. Regis, Montana, on Oct. 7, 2002. Old General Railway Signal Company Model 2A semaphores, installed by the Northern Pacific, still protect trains on the modern day Montana Rail Link.

Photo by Howard Ande
Nikon F5; 80-200mm f2.8 Nikkor zoom lens; Fuji Velvia f5.6 1/320

Making magnificent images is a mix of skill, hard work, and a little luck. On Oct. 5, 2002, Howard Ande caught a slow-moving, Burlington Northern Santa Fe freight crossing the trestle over Lake Pend Oreille west of Sand Point, Idaho, just as rays of sun pierced the overcast evening sky. This photo is about fantastic light and knowing how to use it.

Photo by Howard Ande
Nikon F5; 50mm f1.4 Nikkor lens; Fuji Velvia

Evening, as well as morning, can be the best times to photograph railway architecture and the trains.

Evening and Night

The art of night photography is one of the most difficult to master, but it's perhaps the most rewarding. Night railway photographs can be powerful and dramatic, or subtle, sublime, or abstract.

For most night photography, you'll need a solid tripod and a camera that allows you to open the shutter for long periods. A cable release and flash equipment can also be useful. You can work with moonlight and starlight, as well as various man-made light sources—such as sodium and mercury vapor. Long exposures are necessary, up to 30 seconds or longer. Focus on trains that have stopped if you wish to make equipment photographs.

Alternatively, make photos that convey motion by allowing a train to pass through and illuminate a scene. Photographers like O. Winston Link and Mel Patrick perfected multiple flash systems for making night action shots.

Night action photographers can apply studio photography techniques to railroad work and develop better control over the lighting. Night photography techniques vary greatly, but several practices can assist in producing better night images.

• Working at dawn or dusk, when there is just a hint of color in the sky, can produce a dramatic image. It adds color and detail to a night scene and texture to the sky. It balances image contrast by lessening the extremes between shadows and highlights. If you wait until the sun is well below the horizon, but leave just a faint blue hue, it can create an ethereal effect that yields compelling color images. This unearthly hue is enhanced by the effect of stars in the sky. Modern Fuji Astia, Provia, and other films rated at 100 speed provide excellent results with a night sky.

• When you work without the effects of man-made light, exposures can be difficult to calculate. Most films suffer from reciprocity failure when used for exposures longer than about one second. (See section on reciprocity and film.)

• Keep flare to a minimum. Whether you're working with existing light or long exposures using multiple flash, reduce flare from external light sources. Before you photograph, look at your lens and make sure extraneous light isn't falling on the front element. Flare can ruin a night shot. Use a lens shade or a piece of cardboard above the camera lens to prevent stray light from hitting the front element. Keep the cardboard out of the field of view.

Traditional flash bulbs have been a favorite tool for night photography for decades. Bulbs provide a greater light duration and a warmer tone than electronic flash. The result appears more pleasing. A Burlington Northern GP30 rests at Rochelle, Illinois. This image was made with a long time exposure combined with strategically placed flashes provided by Mike Danneman.

Photo by Brian Solomon
Nikon F3T; 28mm f2.8 AF Nikkor lens; Kodachrome 25

Opposite Page: E-6 process slide films can produce stunning results at twilight. Two Burlington Northern Pacific trains on the Montana Rail Link at the former Northern Pacific station in Helena were captured in a time exposure made on a tripod. Illumination blends sodium and mercury vapor lights with a twilight sky. Flare is minimized by positioning the camera to avoid harsh man-made light from falling on the front lens element.

Photo by Brian Solomon.
Nikon F3T; 35mm PC Nikkor lens; Ektachrome 64X (EPX) exposed @ f4 for 8 seconds

In the last light of the day, the final frame in the camera was exposed—the last photo of a week-long expedition across Pennsylvania, West Virginia, Maryland, Ohio, and Indiana. A South Shore train races toward South Bend, Indiana, on an October 1994 evening.

Photo by Brian Solomon.
Nikormat FTN; 28mm f2.8 AF Nikkor lens; Fujichrome 100 exposed @ f2.8 1/60

Reciprocity Failure and the Film You Use

Reciprocity failure is the reduction of film sensitivity during very long—or very short—exposures. Under normal daylight conditions, reciprocal f-stop and shutter speed combinations are the equivalent of allowing the same amounts of light to reach the film.

For example, f5.6 @ 1/250th second equals f4 @ 1/500th second or f8 @ 1/125th second. Camera settings can be calculated in one stop increments. f4 @ 1/125th second is one stop less than f5.6 @ 1/125th of a second. This isn't true during long exposures. Your meter might say f4 @ 1/15th of a second is equivalent to f22 @ one second, but these exposures aren't necessarily the same.

A film's reciprocity failure results in it being less sensitive at slower speeds. In order to get an exposure equivalent to f4 @ 1/15 with two seconds, you may have to open your aperture to about f11 instead of the calculated f22. It's important to give the camera extra time for night exposures, or the end result will appear underexposed. One way to work around your in-camera meter is to change the film speed. If you're using 100 speed film, change the ISO dial setting from 100 to 50 to effectively double the length of exposure.

Remember to change the ISO setting back before you work in daylight situations or you risk overexposing daylight images.

Modern E6 emulsions suffer less from reciprocity than older films. Kodachrome 25 was a notoriously poor film for very long exposures. Another problem with reciprocity failure is many films experience a significant color shift with long exposures. Manufacturers provide data on reciprocity failure, indicating the amount of exposure increase required in different circumstances, as well as color correction data.

For example, Fuji Astia experiences reciprocity failure with one minute or longer exposures. A one minute exposure will require an extra 1/3 stop increase to compensate for reciprocity. Fuji Velvia 50 experiences reciprocity failure with speeds of four seconds or longer. Fuji recommends a 1/3 stop increase and a 5cc magenta filter for color correction for a four-second exposure. Velvia suffers from more extreme reciprocity failure than the 100 speed Astia.

Fuji's Provia F, also rated at 100 speed, experiences reciprocity failure with speeds over 128 seconds. Only experimentation with the different films and careful visual comparison will demonstrate which film is most effective for night work.

Working with Wide Angles

The wide angle lens is a versatile tool, readily available to the railway photographer. Its special qualities ought to be taken into consideration for effective use when making railway photographs. The nature of wide angle lens design offers greater depth of field than longer lenses.

If a wide angle lens is stopped down to a small aperture (for example f11, f16, or f22), the depth of field will allow objects from several feet to infinity to appear in relative focus. Experiment with a lens on an SLR body using the depth-of-field preview feature. (A button that permits manual lens stopping down while leaving the viewfinder mirror down.) See the range of focus afforded by the lens. The wider the lens focal length, the greater the depth of field.

Another effect of wide angle lens design is image distortion. The severity and type of distortion depends on the specifics of lens design. Many wide angle lenses cause "barrel distortion," which curves the field of view outward from the center, giving straight lines at frame edges a slight curve. This causes a barrel-like effect on the vertical plane.

◁

At 5:50 a.m. on March 14, 1997, the Hale-Bopp comet can be seen in the sky positioned over the signal at the west switch at Solitude—a remote siding east of Green River, Utah. One advantage of some modern films is improved reciprocity. This allows the portrayal of stars in a twilight sky.

Photo by Brian Solomon
Nikon F3HP; 105mm f1.8 Nikkor lens;
Fuji Provia 100 (RDP) exposed @ f2
for 6 to 8 seconds

Lenses using a flat field design correct for the effects of barrel distortion, but must be used on a level so image lines remain parallel. A flat field lens suffers from distortions such as image stretching.

Another common defect is vignetting. This appears as a slight darkening of the image in the corners or as a "hot spot" at the center of the frame. In extreme cases, vignetting will result in a black circle and a tunnel-like effect. Some wide angles suffer from a loss of sharpness at the edges. It is most acute at the widest aperture.

Better wide angles are designed to compensate for various types of distortion, vignetting, and uneven sharpness. They can be much higher-priced lenses.

Carl Zeiss, Leica, and Schneider are among the highest quality wide angles and feature the sharpest overall image, sharp corners, and a minimum of undesirable qualities.

Using a Wide Angle Lens

In locations where your 50mm 'normal' lens never seemed to give you the best view, a 35mm lens, or perhaps a 28mm lens, may be just right.

A great application for a wide angle is in places where mountains, hills, or tall buildings loom near tracks. A longer lens may give a view of a train against a nondescript backdrop, but a 24mm lens might allow you to include the mountain tops. A low trestle over a small river or creek can be captured with a 20mm lens from the creek bed.

A wide angle lens is a great choice for views of the crew at work in their confines, or of the operator in a signal tower. Wide angles also are good inside passenger cars and railway stations.

When using wide angles, especially super wide lenses like the 21mm, 24mm, or 28mm in the 35mm film format, pay close attention to foreground detail. A wide angle lens will feature more of foreground. It will seem more prominent and sharper than it will with longer lenses. Place something of interest in the foreground. Try photographing a grain train rolling through a field of harvested wheat or corn at harvest time.

The wide angle is a good lens to use in spectacular weather. Use your 28mm lens to feature tracks beneath a complex tapestry of clouds. This can be sublime at sunset or sunrise. Sometimes the only sun you might see is for a few minutes at sunrise, when the sky turns deep red. Make the most of it. Watch for a rainbow after a rain and and keep that 24mm handy!

Wide Angle Techniques

If you are photographing moving trains, a faster shutter speed will be needed to stop the motion with a wide angle than is required with longer lenses. Assuming a full-frame, 3/4 angle of a moving train, the wider field of view results in greater relative motion of the train to the film plane.

The shutter speed needed to stop the action will depend on the speed of the train, angle of view, and proximity of the camera to the train. If

A Dublin-bound train approaches Irish Rail's Killucan Cabin just after sunset on May 3, 2002.

Photo by Brian Solomon
**Nikon N90S; 24mm AF Nikkor lens;
Fuji Sensia 100 (RA)**

Opposite Page: When you're committing your favorite trains to film, don't forget to include their environment. Including the whole scene will give the viewer greater information than images of plain trains. On Sept. 13, 2002, the Royal Canadian Pacific luxury train's surroundings give full reason why this train runs.

Photo by Mike Danneman
Pentax ZX-M; 35mm f.2 SMC Pentax-A lens; Fuji Provia 100F (RDP III) exposed @ f8.5 1/250

A super-wide-angle lens is a good tool for making interior photos. This image of Washington Union Station was made with a Hologon flat field 16mm. This lens doesn't exhibit barrel distortion. Avoid severe line convergence by keeping lens level.

Photo by Brian Solomon
Contax G2; 16mm f8 fixed aperture Hologon lens; Fuji Astia 100 (RAP) exposed @ f8 for 1 second

1/250 was enough to stop a train with a 50mm lens (35mm film format), you may need at least 1/500 to stop the action with a 28mm. For these reasons, a wide angle lens may be a good choice to show the motion.

Using a moderate shutter speed will allow a slight blurring of the front of the train. Stopping down to a small aperture will yield a more extreme blur with a train passing through a scene and is most effective when the camera is affixed to a tripod.

A wide angle lens will minimize camera motion. Stopping down to a small aperture will allow the use of a slower speed, which will yield more extreme blurring. Try this with a train passing through a scene. It is most effective when the camera is affixed to a tripod. With a 16mm lens, you might be able to keep the lens sufficiently steady at 1/2 second. If you're working in low light with static subjects, a wide angle lens potentially will allow you to make sharper photographs than a normal lens.

The wide angle lens, shutter speed, and aperture choices can leave a photographer in a quandary. If you stop down to increase your depth of field and put your foreground, middle ground, and background in relative sharpness, you must choose a slower shutter speed. Since you'll need a faster shutter speed to stop the action, a compromise is needed.

Assuming you are photographing in full California sunlight with 100 speed slide film, your "normal exposure" is f11 1/250. With a 28mm, this will give you superb depth of field, however, 1/250 probably is not fast enough to stop an Amtrak train moving at speed.

You can easily change your shutter speed to 1/1000, which will allow you to shoot at f5.6. This is a better compromise and still will afford you reasonable depth of field, while giving you enough shutter speed to freeze the train's motion.

When you organize your composition, keep in mind that wide angle lenses feature the most severe distortion and have the least sharpness at the frame edges. You may not want to place the primary subject too close to the edge.

Note that a wide angle lens will make objects seem further away, and smaller, than a normal lens. Avoid losing your subject in the scene. If you are photographing an immense vista, a wide angle can be a seductive choice, but the train crossing the scene may seem inconsequential in the photograph.

Perspective Control Lenses

A specialized variety of wide angle lens is the perspective control lens. These are available for a few 35mm and medium format cameras. A wide angle image suffers severely from line convergence when the film plane isn't on a parallel plane with the subject.

This effect is obvious when photographing tall buildings, or a low angle shot looking up at a locomotive. Line convergence will make buildings or locomotives appear to be falling away from the

Joel Jensen

"Just forget the rules. Forget what you have been taught," says Joel Jensen, a creative California photographer. "To me, there is no such thing as good light or bad light. Adapt to whatever light is available. It's all good."

"Film is cheap. Why not take a chance? If you see something you think is interesting but are worried about it turning out, take it anyway."

"You can take a mental tally at the end of the day. This shot was great … this shot was great. I try to take as many strong photos as I can in a day. It's business from sunup to sundown, and I have a lot of night stuff, also."

"You know when you have taken a good photo. It may never sell, nobody else may like it, but if you like it, that's all that matters."

"Shoot black and white. It will make you a better color photographer. My 'legends' of photography—Dick Steinheimer, Ted Benson, David Plowden, and Winston Link—are primarily black and white photographers."

"Shoot people … the 'legends' emphasized men and machines."

"I had a godfather who was a brakeman for the Milwaukee Road in Mason City [Iowa], and he might have warmed me up a little bit. My Dad is one of those people who just likes trains and he wouldn't know a C44-9 from an SD40.

Joel Jensen got up early to make the sunrise photo of Santa Fe No. 37561 at Belen, New Mexico, in 1992. Those in the photo are Scott Brittin, chief mechanical officer, and retired Santa Fe engineers Rufus King and George Clous. Jensen used Kodak Ektar 125 color negative film. For maximum control, he printed the negative himself.

Photo by Joel Jensen

Jensen started making railroad photos in 1987 when he came across Union Pacific locomotive 844.

"I saw a big cloud of smoke coming up from the Cheyenne roundhouse, thought it's got to be their steam engine. I followed it to Omaha. I have been hooked ever since."

"It's just you. I can go into photography mode and block out the rest of the world. Don't think about anything else on a photography trip."

He focuses all his attention—especially on depots, highways, and railroads—west of the Mississippi. "The West is … where I enjoy going the most."

"I have been just as happy on the Nevada Northern as shooting the UP Challenger."

He volunteers in Nevada probably eight times a year.

"To me, it is the best place to shoot. If people want to have tips on a place to go, I suggest East Ely."

He manages a custom photo lab, and when making prints, frequently gets spectacular results with color negatives. "I have precise control with an enlarger, and use the same burning and dodging techniques as when making black and white prints."

His distinctive style perhaps is attributable to his graphic arts training at Iowa State University in 1979-83, where he excelled in a photography class.

"I absolutely hated photography but I had to take it for my degree. The third time I took the class, all of a sudden it just clicked. The professor put up a slide of an abstract pile of bricks, in black and white. I realized, 'Now I get it.'

"The professor told me I was the best in the class of 80. To me, it just comes naturally. Once I put the viewfinder up to my eye, the whole world is right there in that viewfinder."

On March 1, 1995, a Chicago Metra train rolls through 'NI' on the Chicago & North Western at West Chicago, Illinois. The extreme contrast of this scene makes a monochromatic image on color slide film. Shooting into the early morning sun captures the glazing left by ice that rained down overnight.

Photo by Howard Ande
Nikon FM-2; 80-200mm f2.8 Nikkor zoom lens; Fuji Velvia; f5.6 1/500

camera. A perspective control lens can help you correct for the convergence of vertical lines by keeping the camera level and adjusting the front element up or down to cover the subject area.

Photographers using large format (4x5 inch film and larger) view-cameras routinely use such adjustments to minimize line convergence. This is common in architectural and commercial product photography, but rarely is used in contemporary railway photography. Several 35mm camera manufacturers have offered perspective control lenses. For example, Nikon has produced both 35mm and 28mm PC lenses.

Perspective control lenses are more costly than conventional wide angles of the same length. They're not as fast. For example, the Nikon 35mm PC's fastest aperture is just f3.5. Nikon makes conventional 35mm lenses two stops faster. PC lenses tend to reduce corner sharpness and are effective with the camera leveled on a tripod.

They can be used to make excellent train photos, especially where significant structures, such as bridges, are involved. The PC lens can be especially useful for photos of railway architecture.

Telephoto Lenses

English lensmaker Thomas Rudolf Dallmeyer patented the telephoto lens in 1891. They were used by professional photographers for many years, and have been offered in the 35mm format by Leitz and others since the 1930s. Few railroad photographers took advantage of them until the early 1960s, when single lens reflex (SLR) cameras and relatively inexpensive telephoto lenses became popular.

"Telephoto" is short for *telephotographic*—to photograph at a distance. A telephoto lens magnifies the perspective and brings distant objects closer. Short telephotos in the 70 to 135mm range have respective factors of magnification from 1.6 to 3.0. A very long telephoto in the 1200mm range has a factor of magnification of about 26.

A telephoto lens causes a perceived foreshortening of distance, which visually compresses a subject. The longer the lens, the greater the magnification, and the more acute the distortion of the linear perspective. The longer a lens, the shallower its depth of field, and the narrower its field of focus. The effect of a telephoto lens can be seen by holding a frame at a distance and looking at the relationships of objects in that frame.

Focusing at a distance, such as when you're driving on a long section of highway, offers you the telephoto lens effect. A telephoto perspective may seem strange presented as an enlarged print in very sharp focus.

A telephoto lens can be valuable for railway photography, but should be used carefully and with discretion. A telephoto lens is best used as a tool to create a composition, not as a crutch because you can't change your viewpoint or as a gimmick to create distortion without some photographic merit.

Working with a Telephoto

A telephoto magnifies a scene—and it magnifies camera vibration. Photos made with longer lenses are more likely to suffer from camera shake. To reduce the effects of camera motion, increase shutter speed or keep your camera steady.

Faster shutter speed only minimizes the effects of camera motion. Increasing shutter speed from 1/250 to 1/500 of a second cuts blur created by camera shake in half. There are techniques to reduce camera movement caused by your heart beating and your nervous system. Hold the end of the lens with one hand and brace your arm with your elbow against your chest to minimize tension. Before you release the shutter, take a deep breath, then let it out to relax your body. Manufacturers like Canon and Nikon now offer image stabilization lenses that automatically correct for nominal vibration. They allow much sharper hand-held telephoto images.

A solid, well-made tripod is the most effective way to minimize camera motion.

A heavy tripod with a well designed head will keep a camera steady. A sturdy tripod can be imperative for making sharp photos with long lenses at slow shutter speeds. Choose carefully. Many tripods on the market are too flimsy for effectively steadying long lenses.

Some tripods, used in combination with cameras with fast motor-drives, suffer from harmonic vibration that actually may decrease your overall image sharpness. You may decide to take long telephoto images without the aid of a motor-drive.

An SLR's mirror bounce causes vibration. Some photographers prefer to use 35mm rangefinder cameras, though this is impractical for very long lenses—beyond about 180mm. Better SLRs have a manual mirror lockup feature. Locking your mirror in advance will reduce camera vibration. This is effective only if you have the camera firmly set on a tripod, focused, and composed in advance of releasing the shutter.

Reduced depth of field with telephotos means you have to pay greater attention when focusing in order to avoid soft subjects. Focusing a long lens in low light can be difficult and requires patience. Autofocus systems can help, but you have to be sure you know where the focus point is on an AF camera.

Telephoto Technique

A telephoto image has its best effect when it isn't obvious it was used. Use a telephoto lens to tighten up a scene, reduce foreground clutter, and bring in an impressive background. A telephoto will allow you to photograph trains against a distant mountain range or cityscape. The background will appear to loom above the train.

Telephoto compression will exaggerate thermal distortion seen on a warm day.

Fred Matthews made this composition on the Canadian Pacific at Banff, Alberta, in 1983. Working with simple elements, he produced a powerful image. The highly polished rails reflect the color of the sky and the clouds add texture.

Photo by Fred Matthews
Pentax Spotmatic; 50mm lens of unknown manufacture; Ektachrome

Opposite Page: A perspective control lens allows you to adjust the front element to keep the film plane perpendicular to the horizon, allowing a wide-angle view without converging line distortion. This large-format technique is used in architectural photography and can apply to railway action photos. A 35mm PC lens was used to make this photo of Amtrak No. 6, the *California Zephyr* on the Southern Pacific at Pinole, California.

Photo by Brian Solomon
Nikon F3T; 35mm PC Nikkor lens; Kodachrome 25 exposed at f4 1/500

At 3:50 p.m. on Feb. 8, 1997, UP westbound mani-
fest train DVROM rounds the curve at mile 22 just
west of Clay, Colorado, on former Rio Grande
trackage, now UP's Moffat Tunnel Sub. At the
time, Rio Grande locomotives regularly were
assigned to this train. This photo was made with a
600mm telephoto lens.

Photographer Joe McMillan offers these tips
when using long telephoto lenses:

• A sturdy tripod is a must.
• Since many 600mm photos are of a train
  approaching the camera, the photographer can
  often get away with shooting at lower shutter
  speeds. As long as the camera and lens are
  securely mounted on a sturdy tripod and the subject
  is approaching the camera location, shutter
  speeds as low as 1/60th can be used successfully.
• Long lenses are best used in the early morning
  hours or in cooler seasons as heat waves
  can distort the image and make focusing
  almost impossible.

"I have used my long lenses in the Arizona and
California deserts with interesting results.
Sometimes the distortion from the heat waves
make for an interesting photo, but sometimes it
can be an unrecognizable blob."

Photo by Joe McMillan

Thermal distortion may reduce sharpness, and to the untrained eye, just may appear as missed focus if it's captured out of context.

A telephoto lens can be used to compress grade effects and make mildly undulating track appear like a roller coaster. If you want to show the effect of a heavily graded line, select a vantage point where the gradient changes and use a long lens to exaggerate the change.

You can use a telephoto lens to make detailed photographs and close-ups of an object separated from its surroundings. Selecting a wide aperture and close focus can help you exaggerate the appearance of the narrow field of focus to set off an object (such as a switch stand lantern) against a soft background.

Creative use of telephoto selective focus can set up dramatic juxtapositions, such as in portraiture. A short telephoto, 85 to 105mm, is a great tool for making "people" pictures. Focus on railroaders' faces, perhaps putting other elements somewhat out of focus in the distance.

A popular, clichéd use of the telephoto lens is the "telemash"—a three-quarter view of a train taken with a long lens. This fills the frame with the train, usually the front of the lead locomotive, and minimizes other elements.

Occasionally, this technique can be used for dramatic effect, but if it's used excessively the effect becomes trite and boring. Unfortunately, American railroad publications went through a period from the mid-1980s until recently where the trite vertical telemash was the standard venue for cover images.

Working with low light, a telephoto can be used for many great effects, limited only by the photographer's imagination.

Use a telephoto from a great height, straight down on a train winding through a narrow canyon or placed low to the ground. Focus on the details of a locomotive or station with rich low light of sunset. Capture the expressions of your friends and fellow photographers as a train blasts past them. The possibilities are limitless!

A north-bound North Shore interurban electric train pauses on a rainy evening at the intersection of 6th and National in Milwaukee, Wisconsin. Notice, the street lights have been blocked carefully to accent the photo while producing minimal flare. This photograph appeared as a center spread in *Trains* magazine.

Photo by Richard Solomon
Rolleiflex Model T; f3.5 Zeiss Tessar lens, Kodak Plus-X film (rated at ASA 80)

Quick Check List

Simple checks you can make to improve your odds of success. Neglecting any one of them can result in missed opportunity. Run through them *before* you need to shoot. When the train enters the scene you will be ready.

- Turn the camera "on."
- Take the lens cap off.
- Make sure the ISO setting matches the film in the camera.
- Check battery level and replace if it's low. Don't wait for the batteries to die.
- Check the amount of film left. Don't be caught on the last frame.
- If you are using a camera with manual advance, wind it.
- If you are using an automatic camera, make sure it is in the desired mode.
- Make sure the self-timer isn't "on."
- Make sure the lens is engaged properly.
- Check to see of the lens is clean.
- Focus/check auto focus.
- Take a sample light reading.
- Insure shutter speed and f-stop settings are correct.
- If you haven't taken a photo in several days/weeks, expose a frame or two and make sure everything is working.

CHAPTER 6

ANALYZING YOUR RESULTS

❋ You've done your homework and made photographs. Now you look at what you've done. Are you happy with your results or can you improve them? Examine your photos for focus, exposure, and composition.

Watch for unwanted defects such as scratches, uneven exposure, fingerprints, blotches, staining, and spots. Every photographer has different criteria for judging his or her work. Read more about some basics you can use to determine quality.

Sharpness and Focus

The most effective way to judge sharpness is to examine negatives and slides with a *loupe* (a small photo magnifier) on an even-source light table. A quality loupe will give you a clearer, sharper view and put you in a better position to accurately judge your work.

We suggest using at least an 8X magnification loupe. For critical focus analysis, you may wish to invest in a 10X or even a 12X loupe.

Ask hard questions. Are your photos sharp? Did you focus properly? Was your equipment in top working order? Be critical in examining your slides for focus. If you're not sure your slides are sharp enough, ask a friend. It never hurts to get a second opinion.

When photos lack sharpness, we say that they are "soft," not "blurry." Blurring denotes motion, rather than optical sharpness. We're assuming rail-photographers are seeking optimal sharpness.

Check image sharpness from corner to corner as well as in the center. If you find your photos

When viewing slides on a daylight-balanced light table, compare slides for exposure and composition. If you have made a sequence of images bracketing exposure, decide which photos work best. Compare your slides with your notes to learn from what you've done.

▽ *Photo by Brian Solomon*

Opposite Page: A light table, color-balanced for daylight, and a good loupe are great tools. Carefully examine each slide for composition, sharpness, exposure, and technical defects. Scrutiny with a high-powered loupe is more effective than casual viewing on a slide screen. Use a high quality 8x loupe to examine sharpness.

Photo by Brian Solomon
Contax G2; 16mm f8- fixed aperture Hologon lens; Fuji Astia 100 (RAP) time exposure with bounce fill flash at f8 2 seconds

A CSX auto rack train at Doe Gully on the Magnolia Cutoff east of Paw, West Virginia, on October 18, 1994. Working with telephoto lenses in low light can make it difficult to focus. Carefully view these images to see if you placed your focus point optimally.

Photo by Brian Solomon
Nikormat FTN; 200mm f4 Nikkor lens; Fujichrome 100 exposed @ f4 1/250

At 10:03 a.m. on March 22, 1991, Southern Pacific's Jordan spreader clears the number 2 track at Yuba Pass, California. This image was made in bright Sierra sun. The sky was filled with hazy clouds and a circular polarizing filter was used to reduce the effect of glare and reflection, reducing contrast.

Photo by Brian Solomon
Nikon F3T; 35mm PC Nikkor lens; Kodachrome 25 exposed @ f4.5 1/250 with circular polarizing filter

Opposite Page: Zürich-bound *Cisalpino* at Göschenen, Switzerland. Picking the best exposure to photograph a clean, white train in freshly fallen snow at noon on a clear sunny day is not easy. Relying on an in-camera meter can result in underexposure of snow, since many in-camera meters use an averaging system based on 18 percent gray. In these situations, picking an exposure from past experience or using an 18 percent gray card will offer a better result. Notice, there is texture in the snow and a slight color difference between the snow and the train.

Photo by Brian Solomon
Nikon N90S; 24mm f2.8 AF Nikkor lens; Fuji Sensia II exposed @ f11 1/500

Equipment Testing

Are you suffering from camera difficulties and unsure about the cause of the problem? When you're in the field making photographs of moving trains in constantly changing environments, it can be very difficult to isolate camera problems. By testing your equipment in a controlled environment, you can keep variables to a minimum and quickly isolate technical flaws.

One way to check for shutter problems is to fix your camera and lens on a tripod, make calculated exposure sequences and take detailed notes that will allow you to compare camera setting information directly with processed images. Depending on the nature of the problem, you may find that a front-lit, full-daylight situation works best.

If you're suffering from a lack of sharpness and you suspect a lens problem, set the camera so it is level and facing a distinct, unmoving object. An evenly lit wall that is exactly parallel to the film plane is ideal. Without adjusting composition, run through a full gamut of apertures starting with the lowest. Use equivalent combinations. For example: f2.8 1/2000, f4 1/1000, f5.6 1/500, f8 1/250, f11 1/250, and f16 1/125. You will see how a potential sharpness problem is affected by the aperture size. Do not adjust focus between these exposure variations.

In another test, make a similar set of exposures while focusing on objects at various distances from the camera.

Three sets of exposures should be enough. One set should be a close-focus object. Another should be set at medium distance. The last set should feature an object at the camera's "infinity" focus setting.

For comparison purposes, make at least one set of exposures with another lens—preferably one with characteristics similar to the lens you are testing. If you are using an autofocus camera, you may wish to run comparison tests in various autofocus and manually focused modes. If you normally use a UV or "skylight" filter, make exposure sequences with and without the filter. Note which exposures include the filter. Promptly process the film—the same day if possible—so you may analyze these results as quickly as possible. Other tests, such as those designed to reveal shutter problems, may best be conducted against an evenly-lit white wall, or a clear blue sky. Tests can reveal a variety of potential flaws that may exist with your equipment.

Around the turn of the 20th century, William Bullard used a bulky view camera plus slow dry plates with a daylight exposure of about f8 at two seconds. His lens had flaws and defects, yet look at this photograph!

This view portrays the old Worcester, Massachusetts, Union Station prior to 1911. Bullard adjusted his camera to keep the film plane parallel with the verticals to prevent line convergence. The image is vignetted at the top. The slow film speed meant he couldn't stop the action and people have blurred. These impediments didn't discourage Bullard from producing a priceless collection of period railroad photos.

Photo by William Bullard,
courtesy of Dennis LeBeau

Check for these things:

- Focus point sharpness on a specific object.
- Uniform, corner-to-corner sharpness.
- Hazy or diffused highlights.
- Exposure consistency between frames of equivalent exposure settings.
- Even exposure within each frame.
- Light or dark streaks that weren't part of the scene.
- Vignetting. (A circular darkening in corners.)
- Other flaws, such as barrel distortion, scratches, and incomplete winding.

If you identify a flaw, use your notes and logic to isolate the conditions when the problem appears. If a flaw only appears with one lens, and not with others, the lens is suspect. If a flaw appears only at one f-stop, or only at one shutter speed setting, those settings may be suspect.

A second round of tests may be necessary to further isolate flaws. If you find all exposures are affected, the camera may be suspect. Keep in mind, some defects (such as shutter pinholes and front element lens abrasions) only may become apparent in direct sun settings.

If you conclude your equipment is flawed, you have several options:

1. Continue using the equipment and work around the problem. You risk suffering from flawed photos when you know you could have had better results. This may be necessary as a short-term solution. It's not recommended as a long-term practice.

2. Bring the equipment for repair, assuming it is cost effective. Repairs may not solve an intermittent defect. You may find the problem continues to plague your photography. The effectiveness of repairs depends on many factors, including the competence of the repair person and the severity of the problem.

3. Replace flawed equipment. In situations involving serious and/or intermittent lens flaws, this often is your best option. If the equipment has sentimental value, treat it the same way railroads treat obsolete historic locomotives. Preserve it, but don't use it in daily service.

Some problems, especially intermittent ones, may not be solved by testing. These include minor light leaks, sticky shutters, electronics failures, film jams, and metering difficulties.

In these situations, you may wish to bring photo examples that show the problems along with the suspect equipment when you visit a qualified camera repair shop. Or you may move directly to replacing the flawed equipment.

Do not allow repeatable, persistent, intermittent, or other problems to cause you to miss photographs.

aren't sufficiently sharp, you must determine what causes the softness. If you find you're consistently getting soft images, action is required. You must determine whether your soft photos are the result of photographer error or equipment failure.

A common problem is missed focus. Using a manual focus lens, you may inadvertently miss your optimal focus point. Even skilled photographers do this.

Routine difficulties focusing, particularly with long lenses, may mean problems with your camera or your lens. You may need glasses or contact lens upgrading.

The longer the lens, the more critical focus becomes. Photographs made with longer lenses require special attention, since it's easier to be out of focus.

When you photograph a train head-on with a long telephoto lens, the ideal is to focus on the front of the train. If this isn't done carefully, the focus point may fall in front or behind the nose of the train.

It takes practice and skill to quickly focus on a moving subject. Some photographers prefer to pre-focus on a desired point and release the shutter when the train comes into focus. This may be easiest when the camera is fixed on a tripod.

If you use a camera in autofocus mode, never assume it will necessarily select the best focus position. Autofocus is a tool, and not magic. It must be used properly to obtain the best results. Despite the best technology, sometimes an autofocus camera will miss. Yet, autofocus is a valuable option for those who have difficulty focusing. If you are consistently getting out-of-focus photographs, try an autofocus system.

Low light situations exacerbate focus and sharpness problems. In low light, the widest apertures (low f-stop settings) often are necessary to use the fastest possible shutter speeds. A wider aperture results in lower depth of field and a narrower field of focus. That can appear to exaggerate missed focus.

Depth of field relates to the size of the aperture and length of the lens. The smaller the aperture (or higher "f" number), the greater the depth of field. The longer the lens, the lower the depth of field.

Lenses may exhibit flaws when used at their widest apertures. Even high quality lenses are sharpest toward the middle of their f-stop range. Low light situations present problems. Low contrast can make it difficult for your eyes to focus properly. Some autofocus cameras also may have difficulties in low contrast situations.

An AF camera that hunts for focus at the moment you want to release the shutter can cause you to miss the optimal shot.

Two images portray Southern Pacific's Jordan spreader clearing Donner Pass at Norden, California, after a heavy snow storm. Although back-lit, the snow reduces harshness of the shadows. By carefully exposing for the snow, both photos retain detail in the highlights and shadows despite difficult lighting. The snow exposure was 1.5 stops down from the normal daylight exposure without snow. Shading the lens to avoid direct sunlight falling on the front element avoided unwanted flare.

Photo by Brian Solomon
Nikon F3T; 200mm f4 Nikkor lens;
Kodachrome 25 exposed @ f8 1/250

Opposite Page: This detailed view of grass and flowers at Grodzisk, Poland, demonstrates the effect of a telephoto lens with low depth of field. Using a wide aperture, the plane of focus is very narrow. Sometimes this effect is desirable. However, if you miss your point of optimal focus, you may find the subject that you intended to be sharp comes out soft. To obtain greater depth of field, use a smaller aperture (higher f-number).

Photo by Brian Solomon
Nikon N90S; 180mm f2.8 ED Nikkor lens;
Fuji Sensia (RA) exposed @ f2.8 1/500

Is Your Equipment Flawed?

If you have ruled out user failure as a cause of unwanted softness, the next step is to determine if your equipment is flawed. Even the best equipment can fail.

Vibrations from traveling and rough handling can loosen lens elements, camera mounts, mirrors, focusing prisms, and other key components. A good lens can develop a loose element and become unacceptably soft with little warning.

You may not be able to detect lens problems through the viewfinder. These problems only become apparent in your results. A loose element or lens mount can result in a problem that can be frustrating to locate. Common lens problems include scratches or dirt. Glass fungus often grows slowly on lens elements. Scratches can be troublesome and may result in hazy highlight areas. Carefully test equipment in a controlled environment.

Experiment by running comparison tests using different camera and lens combinations. Vary the f-stops and take careful notes.

Using telephoto lenses requires careful attention to focus. On April 26, 2002, a PKP (Polish State Railways) 2-8-2 Mikado Class Pt47 switches the yard at Wolzstyn, Poland.

Photo by Brian Solomon
Nikon N90S; 180mm f2.8 ED Nikkor lens;
Fuji Sensia (RA)

Brian Plant

"Find a way to relax while you are taking railroad photographs," suggests Brian Plant, who has been an especially creative photographer since he started college in 1999.

"There is nothing more relaxing than sitting around a campfire at trackside, listening to crickets and a train approaching from 20 miles away."

Born in 1981, Plant has been taking photographs since he was six. At first he made wedge shots using a 50mm lens, with the sun at his back. The early start, plus the inspiration from 1960s photos by Jeremy F. Plant, his father, influenced him to try different approaches.

"Now, I am trying to capture the mood of the scene."

That lends itself to working much of the time at night and at twilight. When he's trying to capture the differing qualities of moon and sunlight, Brian works a lot with signals, bridges, and broad landscapes. He also likes to photograph in the mist and rain.

"I am looking for something that doesn't lead to what might be considered a normal photo. Anything that captures my eye I will try and photograph."

A student at Ithaca College, he says classes there influenced his outlook, but says his friends' ideas have been equally important. He mentions being encouraged by doing photographs with M. Ross Valentine, Peter Furneé, and Mel Patrick, among others.

In March 2001 he and Valentine were taking photos of Baltimore & Ohio signals at night on Sand Patch Grade in the bitter cold.

"It proved to me how exciting and enjoyable it was when taking railroad photos at night."

One month later, he met Furneé.

"At the time, Peter was sort of in a rut. We created a bond, going out together on short trips. I got him interested in night photography again … that led to a joint effort emulating the past night work of O. Winston Link and Mel Patrick utilizing synchronized flash bulbs."

Plant uses film cameras, mostly with Fuji slide film and E-6 color processing. He uses black and white negatives but makes extensive use of computer technology to scan and post photos on the Internet.

"Having equipment that allows you to photograph the way you want is important, but a Nikon F5 wouldn't let the worst photographer be the next Galen Rowell or Richard Steinheimer."

Recently, he started an e-mail discussion group to attract young photographers. Brian wants to find people he might have things in common with and is interested in forming bonds that will promote the next generation of railroad photographers.

Brian's photos have appeared in *Trains, CTC Board, Railroad Explorer,* and *Railfan & Railroad* magazines.

"Shoot full," Plant concludes.

To quote photographer Richard Steinheimer, Plant explains "… one should capture the whole railroad scene, not just the pretty scenery and engines. This might include signals, the terrain a railroad passes through, the employees on the railroad, etc. …"

"Don't be afraid to take a picture or to do something different. Look to other people for inspiration. Find something you enjoy. Don't just settle for what people are telling you to do."

The shape of railroading at Leipsic Jct., Ohio, is relatively unchanged from days past. The classic Nickel Plate signals and code line remain, as well as the abandoned tower protecting the crossing with the former B&O Cincinnati-Toledo mainline. One can use night light to dramatize elements such as the signals and code line depicted here.

Photo by Brian Plant
Nikon F100; 300mm f4 AF-ED Nikkor lens; Provia 400F (RHP) exposed at f5.6 for 30 seconds

Exposure

Exposure separates good photographs from mediocre ones. Proper exposure is opinion—a matter of how the photo looks to the person judging it and how the photo is used. Photos are judged differently for publication than for personal use.

Analyzing exposure is judging image density. An image that isn't dense enough appears too light. It is 'overexposed'—received too much light. If the image is too dense, it appears dark. It is "underexposed"—didn't receive enough light.

If you keep careful notes, you'll learn from successes and failures and get a better feeling about exposing your photos. Film types respond differently to varied lighting situations.

Slide Film

Slide films are "positive" materials making exposure analysis more direct. Both black and white and color print films are "negative" materials (why the processed film is called a "negative") so the principles for judging exposure are reversed. These descriptions assume that slides depict standard front-lit scenes. Unusual scenes or those featuring extreme contrast or unusual lighting have different exposure criteria. Exposure increments are measured in f-stops. This applies both in the field and in assessment of the image.

Assuming the film has been processed properly, and the images depict a normally lit scene, the exposures are measured in f-stops in the field and as you assess the image.

With a one stop increase, the amount of light reaching the film is doubled. A stop decrease halves the amount of light reaching the film. The sensitivity of most films is limited to 1/3 stop increments, although most cameras only show full-stop increments.

Latitude describes the amount of exposure tolerance a film has between the lightest areas

Opposite Page: Two images of the same train at the same place. With the cooperation of New England Central, and through the special help of the railroad's locomotive engineer, Steve Carlson, the train was posed on a trestle at New London, Connecticut. The top image was photographed from a tight angle with a 24mm, while the bottom image was taken from ground level capturing the reflection of the train in the water. Which is the better shot?

Photo by Brian Solomon
Tech data for top photo: 7-9 Nikon N90S; 24mm f2.8 Nikkor lens; Fuji Provia (RDP) Tech data for bottom photo: 7-10 Nikon N90S; 24mm f2.8 Nikkor lens; Kodachrome 25

At Right and Below: Chicago's Union Station opened in 1925. It is an example of a grand structure seen every day by passengers and photographers. For a station of its scope, photos are spare. Perhaps that's a reason *Trains* editor David P. Morgan asked John Gruber to photograph the station and its people in 1964. Gruber spent three days at the station to make the story, which appeared in a 13-page photo essay in 1965. Two selections appear here. Rays of sun pour into the station's concourse, demolished in 1969 and replaced by a high-rise building. And passengers from a Gulf, Mobile and Ohio train hurry into the station. Today, it truly is a "union station" since all of Amtrak's intercity trains use it.

Photos by John Gruber

Little Valley, California, located at MP 108 on the BNSF Gateway Subdivision, once was a bustling, small community that supplied regular loads of finished lumber to the Western Pacific RR. The silence is broken by the faint rumble of a quartet of BNSF locomotives as they attack the steep grade out of the Pit River Valley south of Bieber. The big question is whether the HVBCBAR will make it to our location before the sun sets. With less than 10 minutes of light to spare, the AT&SF 856, BNSF 4666, BNSF 8212, and BNSF 4484 thunder through Little Valley at 7:50 p.m. As we prepare our dinner we can hear the 856 and mates climb for what seems an eternity in this land of peace and quiet.

Photo by Kevin Dorn
Mamiya 645 1000s; Mamiya 210mm f4 lens; Kodak Tri-X 400 (rated at ASA 200) exposed @ f8 1/500sec; developed in Ilford ID 11 developer; printed on Ilford Multigrade IV RC Deluxe paper.

Dorn Family

The Dorn family is making its mark on railroad photography in California. While Dick and son, Kevin, a high school senior, talked about their photographic experiences at Winterail 2003, another son, Justin, was studying for classes at University of California-Davis. Dick and Justin have won awards at the annual event. Kevin is beginning to enter photos.

Dick put cameras in his sons' hands when they were young.

"What really was effective for me was sharing quality time with them."

"Having a dad who is interested makes it real easy for you to follow," says Kevin. "It's tougher for kids when they have to do it on their own."

Dick started taking his sons on photo outings with instructions from their mother, Chris, to bring them home safely—or not come home!

Justin had a camera when he was 8 or 9. Once Kevin got a camera, at age 12, his approach to rail fan trips changed.

"He became a more serious photographer. I talked to them a lot about composition and exposure. They picked it up fast," Dick says.

Kevin shoots a lot on his own, mostly around Yuba City, California, where the Dorns have lived since 1971. Dick teaches third graders there.

Dick first held a 35mm camera in 1962 as a high school sophomore and member of a Walnut Creek, California, model railroad group.

"The very first picture I took was in Marysville of the *California Zephyr* and one of the Sacramento Northern juice jacks. Now that I have lived in the Yuba City-Marysville area for 32 years that has real meaning to me."

He started college in 1964 and when he found a dark room, he began to explore black and white photography.

From 1969 to 1976, he shot black and white exclusively. Since then, he has done color slides with a 35mm camera and black and white negatives with a Mamiya 645 medium format camera.

When he started shooting, he picked up books like Dick Steinheimer's *Backwoods Railroads of the West,* and looked at pictures that appealed to him.

"… look at photographers you admire. See how they do things. But, take the kind of pictures you enjoy taking."

Dorn and Steinheimer have collaborated on a book about Donner Pass.

Kevin, who works mainly in black and white, adds:

"You can work with it in the dark room and make it do what you want. You can make your print exposure a little longer or a little shorter or burn stuff in. If you don't have your exposure right for color, there is no fixing it."

Kevin likes photographs to have good light and a nice location.

"On the High Line, there are places where you can see a train in the mountains. I look at some pictures and think, OK, it's a nice picture of a train, but expand on it," Kevin says.

"People shoot tight a lot. It's nice to see what is behind the engines, too."

(highlights) and the darkest areas (shadows.) When texture is lost in *highlights*, they are overexposed or "washed out." When texture is lost in the *shadows*, they are "blocked up." A properly exposed photo balances highlights and shadows.

Shadow areas in a locomotive photo—such as trucks and components on the machine's dark side—may not be too severely affected by a one-stop overexposure. Headlights, windows, and lightly-painted areas may be washed out. The sky will be badly affected by overexposure. Most modern E6 films (Fujichrome, Ektachrome, or Agfachrome) normally can tolerate about 1/2 stop overexposure without significant loss of detail in highlight areas.

With E6 films, underexposed slides can appear to be muddy. That isn't necessarily true with Kodachrome films, which tolerate small amounts of underexposure. While E6 films have color dyes in the emulsion at the time of exposure, Kodachrome film has three layers of black and white film with the colored dyes added in processing.

Color saturation is built into the E6 film while Kodachrome color saturation is exposure-sensitive. Reducing exposure increases color saturation. Some photographers underexpose Kodachrome between 1/3 to 1/2 stops in order to produce a "fully saturated" slide. The slides look great on a screen, but reproduce poorly in books and magazines.

Decide whether to lean toward overexposure or underexposure. An overexposed photo of a silver Amtrak train in bright daylight will suffer greater loss of detail than an overexposed photo of a black Norfolk Southern coal train on a dull day.

It's better to lean toward *underexposure* of lighter subjects, and to lean toward *overexposure* of darker ones. In order to get better detail on the side of a brightly lit Amtrak train, the sky may appear darker. The sky may look washed out with the Norfolk Southern coal train.

An Irish Rail cement train near Tipperary town, Ireland, on May 11, 2000.

Photo by Brian Solomon
Nikon N90S; 105mm f1.8 Nikkor lens;
Fuji Sensia II

Print Film

Photographs made with print films are more tolerant of exposure error. There are two primary reasons for this. First, print films have greater exposure latitude than slide films. Second, since a negative is used as intermediary, adjustments and corrections can be made in the final photograph.

In judging exposure of negatives, remember the principles are reversed. An overexposed slide appears too light and an overexposed negative will appear too dark. Print films are more tolerant of overexposure. A photo that has received one stop too much light can be corrected easily in printing.

However, an underexposed negative is more difficult to correct. When exposing negatives, it is better to lean toward overexposure than risk underexposure.

In judging color prints, signs of underexposure are shadows that seem grayish and grainy with low overall color saturation. Underexposed black and white negatives will appear very light and lacking detail. Extremely overexposed color negatives can result in a loss of highlight detail as well as a color shift, while black and white negatives will seem very dense. That will increase granularity in the final print. The art of obtaining an ideal black and white negative and print has been the subject of numerous books and publications. While we don't have the space for a detailed discussion of the back and white process, one formula for making pleasing and richly toned black and white photos is to overexpose the negatives one stop and under process the film accordingly. Doing this effectively takes practice, patience, and lots of experimentation.

The Rio Grande Ski Train climbs the Front Range at Coal Creek, Colorado, at 8:15 a.m. on March 8, 2003. Bright sun and clean train make for a perfect photo opportunity.

Photo by Tom Mangan
Canon EOS 1v; 70-200mm f2.8 zoom lens;
Fuji Provia 100F (RDP III) exposed @ f5.6 1/800

Ted Benson

Get a simple camera and learn the basics. Look at other people's work for ideas, advises Ted Benson, a full-time newspaper photographer since 1970.

"I suggest trying to get the simplest possible camera, preferably all manual. Learn how to set shutter speeds and f-stops. Read a light meter. You need a good rudimentary background on how to make a simple photograph."

For a beginning photographer, Benson recommends shooting color just to get the camera operation down.

"You are not going to have the dynamic of lab time and processing on top of the camera operation," says Benson.

"Black and white is a very labor-intensive path to take but you have a lot more control. You can shoot where color would not even be worth trying."

Benson's first 35 years of railroad photography are summarized in *One Track Mind*, published in 2000 by Boston Mills.

He studies other photographers' images.

"My early idols were Richard Steinheimer, Phil Hastings, Robert Hale, Parker Lamb, and [John Gruber]. You pick up different things from different photographers. Donald Duke is straightforward, but tries to find some kind of framing. That was one thing I emulated. The more you expose yourself to high quality photography, the more ideas you are going to come up with. I could think of two dozen photographers whose styles I have incorporated at one time or another."

The photojournalism degree he received in 1970 has been helpful.

"A lot of 'people' photography is based on getting folks to relax and be comfortable with you in their presence—in essence, forgetting you are there."

"I try to respect people's working areas. If they don't want their picture taken, that is the way it is. I live with it," says Benson. "More often than not, railroad workers or passengers are good with pictures."

For the newspaper, the work has been 100 percent digital since 2001.

"Digital is not what I do for fun, relaxation, and artistic expression. I have spent 35 plus years as a photographer shooting traditional film and you don't change overnight."

"For people who are traditionally trained, like I am, it is a case of making digital work for you … the same thing with traditional photography."

"It may be a cliché to say that the camera is a tool, but the camera is a tool. It doesn't matter how you get there—what matters is the image. Sometimes pictures are obvious, sometimes situations aren't obvious."

"I can't expect to go down to Tehachapi and take a picture that Bob Hale, Dick Steinheimer, or Stan Kistler took 40 years ago. Some of the landscape has changed; the railroad certainly has changed. You get an idea of how somebody would approach any given situation. It's a starting point. The end point is whatever you make of it."

San Jose Station during the last week of Southern Pacific-operated commutes, June 4, 1985.

Photo by Ted Benson

CHAPTER 7   PUBLISHING YOUR PHOTOS

PUBLISHING YOUR PHOTOS

❋ A Myth

Satisfied with recent results, you decide to make your first submission for publication. You select a favorite slide, tenderly wrap it, write a polite letter "To the Editor" of a glossy railway publication, and send it off.

Two days later, the editor opens your letter and is thrilled to receive the slide. He stops the press and places your photo on his magazine's cover. Within hours he calls to congratulate you and sends a check for $1,000.

You become the envy of your friends and railroad photographers everywhere. You are asked to give presentations and international publishers hound you for your stunning railway images. While such an episode is possible, it is improbable.

An Unfortunate Scenario

A railway photographer sends a newsworthy photo off to his favorite magazine. It portrays an unusual locomotive leading a train on a local mainline. The photographer thinks his photo is newsworthy because of the unusual locomotives. He mistakenly believes the editors will intuitively recognize the significance of the image and will immediately publish it in the next issue.

Three weeks pass, the photographer eagerly rips open his copy of the magazine and leafs through the pages looking for his name and photo. He reaches the back cover and is disappointed. He waits patiently for the next issue, only to be disappointed again. Four months later, the magazine returns his slide with a form rejection notice.

Feeling like a spurned young lover, anger builds in the photographer's heart and he vows never to send *that* magazine another photo. Eventually he abandons the hobby.

The magazine staff didn't see the significance of the photo, is oblivious to his anger, and goes on publishing photographs as they have for years.

Getting In

Publishing your work can be satisfying and rewarding. Seeing your work on a magazine's glossy pages can make your efforts worthwhile. Just as establishing a good strategy for making photos improves your odds of producing successful images, a well-conceived publishing strategy will improve the odds of getting your photos in print.

A practical strategy includes regularly producing high quality work. You need to anticipate the

Opposite Page: Against all odds, Richard Steinheimer produced a spectacular series of photographs in December 1973 of the Milwaukee Road's electrified route out of Avery, Idaho. He rode the nose of the diesel immediately behind motor E77, a powerful Little Joe, making 30 second exposures with the full moon providing an incredibly bright nocturnal landscape. He had only two rolls of Tri-X film, 24 frames, to make what may well be the most memorable photos of his long career. One view of Second Train 262 climbing St. Paul Pass is reproduced here.

Photo by Richard Steinheimer

A Norfolk Southern RoadRailer at South Fork, Pennsylvania, in March 2001. Low winter sun offers soft lighting. A wide-angle pan, exposed at 1/15 second, conveys power. A wide-angle lens with a slow-speed pan gives a band of sharp focus. A dozen frames were exposed to get this image— the opening photo for an article in *Trains* magazine.

Photo by Brian Solomon
Nikon N90S; 24mm f2.8 Nikkor lens;
Fuji Provia 100F (RDP-III) film;
f-stop not recorded at 1/15th of sec

editors' needs. Submit your work regularly in a professional fashion and provide simple, accurate captions. Keep realistic expectations and be patient.

Role as Photo Supplier

As a contributor, you are supplying materials to a railway magazine and you are competing with many other suppliers of similar materials. An editor is the procurer of these materials. The editor's job is to provide his readers, the consumers, with interesting articles and photos, rewarding magazine buyers with the best, most appropriate material.

It's important to understand this relationship. As a supplier in a very competitive market, your product must be *more* appealing than your competition. The visual quality of your images is one of the parameters needed to convince an editor to select your product. You can do several things to make your work more appealing.

1) Anticipate what the editor wants.
2) Get it on the editor's desk when it's needed.
3) Ensure the photographs are adequately captioned.
4) Explain why your photographs are significant.
5) Don't place unrealistic or unnecessary demands on the editor.

Time and Content

A magazine editor's most precious commodity is time. He never has enough. Try to save the editor's time. If you can read the editor's mind, you are saving his or her time.

You don't need to be psychic. Pay close attention to the magazine. Take a look at the types of photos used and analyze how you can provide those images. Observe the subjects portrayed, the treatment, as well as the placement and who has provided images.

A railway magazine isn't looking for just *any* railway photo. They often specialize in the types of subject matter and the manner it is presented. Some magazines prefer photos of modern freight trains rolling through spectacular scenery. Others focus on historic images of steam locomotives, or contemporary views of railway museums.

General interest magazines may combine a variety of elements. Most magazines illustrate sections in different ways. Feature sections usually contain articles on specific topics. News sections will feature recent images relating to current topics, yet news photos often stand on their own.

Other magazines occasionally run photo galleries that feature superlative photography. Sometimes they're the work of one photographer, and other times they feature many photographers'

A cold day in New York's lower Hudson Valley made a stunning photographic setting. A New York-bound Empire Corridor train crosses the causeway between Roa Hook and Peekskill shortly after sunrise on November 20, 1992. In the mid-1990s, video-producer Pentrex published this clean, bright photograph on the rear cover of a video jacket.

Photo by Brian Solomon
Nikon F3T; 200mm f4 Nikkor lens;
Kodachrome 25 exposed @ f4 1/500

Opposite Page: This classic view of the New York Central in the lower Hudson River Valley near the Bear Mountain Bridge has appeared in *Passenger Train Journal* and several books. In 1963, it was typical of New York Central operations and could have been made any day of the week. In just a few years, New York Central and its E-units were just memories. Today, this view is a classic.

Photo by Richard Jay Solomon
Leica M3, 50mm f2 Summicron lens;
Kodachrome

works. In recent years, some magazines have run 'themed photo galleries' or grouped photos portraying a common theme. They may take a seasonal approach such as an autumn color gallery in October.

Contests are another gallery, advertised months in advance, and usually are open to all. They may feature a theme. The advantages to photo contests are the deadlines and subject matter are advertised. Editors will review all the material in a timely fashion and, if it's published, you will get more attention than an ordinary submission. Yet, the competition for each published image is greater than it is for general submissions.

Style

Photographic style is important. Generally, magazine editors don't feature photographs they feel are unworthy of publication. Since every editor has his/her preferences, published photo styles vary greatly from publication to publication.

A locomotive journal that normally publishes standard three-quarter views of unusual locomotive

Finding new and creative ways to portray a common subject can attract an editor's eye. This telephoto silhouette of an L-Taraval street car in San Francisco is simple and graphic. The image fulfills a stereotype of hilly San Francisco without being a total cliché. *Passenger Train Journal* ran this image in issue 210, published in 1995.

Photo by Brian Solomon
Nikon F3T; 200mm f4 Nikkor lens; Kodachrome 25

Jim Boyd

"Learning to look for photo credits is something some people tumble to right away. I learned to become familiar with photo credits when I was in Milwaukee in the 1960s. To this day, I can recognize photographers by their styles," says Jim Boyd, editor of *Railfan* (later, *Railfan & Railroad*) from 1974 to 1997.

Boyd was in Milwaukee to take a two-year photography course in 1962 and 1963 at the Layton School of Art. During that time, he was on a first-name basis with David P. Morgan, *Trains* editor. He spent the few extra dollars he had to buy a "fistful" of back issues with each visit to Morgan's office at 1027 No. Seventh Street. Those magazines inspired Boyd to look for the credit lines and creative photographs.

He got to know Russ Porter at "Monday Night Slide Group"—which met on Tuesday.

"Russ taught me to write magazine articles."

Boyd then had articles published in *Railroad Model Craftsman* in 1964.

"Hal (Carstens, the editor) published all I sent him for *RMC*, because Russ showed me how to send a complete package."

While he was in school, Boyd had concluded that rail fan activity was expensive. Magazine articles turned it into a productive hobby.

Boyd also worked at a portrait studio and TV station. While a field instructor for Electro-Motive Division, from 1967 to '70, he copied most of the surviving diesel locomotive color styling drawings originated at La Grange.

After a year on the Illinois Central, he worked for Carstens Publications, initially as an associate editor for *Flying Models*. He and *RMC* editor Tony Koester started *Railfan* as a quarterly in fall of 1974. It took over *Railroad Magazine* in 1979.

The renamed *Railfan & Railroad* went monthly in September 1987. As editor through October 1997, Boyd became known for lighting night flash photos. The largest was in 1979 in Washington, D.C., when he set up equipment for 100 people for a night photo of eight tracks of locomotive fronts—a football field of trains.

Boyd started in 1953 at age 12 with a Brownie Hawkeye photograph of an Illinois Central Mikado. He published the photo in his book, *Monday Mornin' Rails*. While he attended the University of Illinois for three semesters, he met graduate student J. Parker Lamb. Lamb sold Boyd cameras and taught him how to take train pictures.

Today, Boyd writes columns for *Railfan & Railroad* and *Railroad Model Craftsman*. He carefully explains the potential of digital photography and expects that within a year, good quality digital cameras will be in the realm of the average rail fan.

"Kodachrome 25 snobs will have to become memory chip snobs," he jokes.

"Think about your interests and how to market your photos," Boyd advises.

"Ask yourself, 'Why am I getting into this?' If it is because you like trains, do your best to capture them. Criticize your stuff without criticizing yourself. Your photography [will have] a sense of purpose it would not otherwise have."

Magazine articles gave Boyd a mission and a satisfying way of using the photographs.

"Putting them together in magazine articles or books and seeing that work laid out in front of me is neat. I can see it put to its ultimate use and preserved."

A Delaware & Hudson General Electric U30C rolling through Treichlers, Pennsylvania, in mid-July 1977. Boyd used a 50mm normal lens on a Nikon F. A shutter speed of 1/500th of a second stopped the action on Kodachrome 64.

"Jeff Schaumburg was riding with his dad Bill and me," says Boyd. "I sent him down the street where his red outfit perfectly matched the adjacent barn as he waved at the engine. I love the complexity of the lighting and the buildings and the effectiveness of the framing."

Photo by Jim Boyd

types probably wants to publish more of the same. Sending your pre-dawn photos of freight cars rolling through deep snow is a waste of everyone's time.

A magazine that features cutting-edge photography probably won't be interested in cleanly lit, three-quarter views of the latest locomotive to roll out of the shop. A creatively exposed view of the same machine might be just what they are looking for.

One way to measure an editor's photo preferences is by looking at the largest feature photos. A photo given priority placement indicates the magazine staff likes the image. Pay close attention to the subject, style, and treatment—what they liked about it.

This can greatly help in the preparing your submission. Look at the angle of presentation, the overall size of the subject in proportion to the image, lighting, and other elements that make the photo.

Is it in a rural or urban setting? Are there people in the photo? Does the photo feature creative use of foreground and background? Is it a "high impact" photo, or a more subtle image? If a magazine always features "in your face," high impact photos with bright colors and strong lighting, don't send them subtle images.

Editors may be unconscious to the exact qualities that typify images in their magazines. They know what they like when they see it, but can't articulate those qualities. If you can quantify the images they tend to print, you will have a decided advantage over other contributors.

Do you want to be known for your own style or do you settle for fulfilling someone else's vision? It's nice to see your images in print, and you can learn what various editors like. Your best course may be to establish your own published style. This takes time, patience, and the ability to visually coax editors into using your work.

After you've published a few photos, you'll have a better idea what editors want. Use that

knowledge to shape future contributions. Decide whether to send editors a variety of different images of the same subject and let them choose one to run, or narrow the selection and encourage an editor to embrace your vision.

A number of technical considerations are used to select a photo for publication that can affect an editor's judgment. That choice may be influenced by how well an editor or art director feels a photo will look in print.

Magazines and books normally prefer slides, traditionally the standard medium for color reproduction. There are several good reasons for this. Transparencies tend to offer greater contrast range than print materials, and offer sharper reproduction. The reproduction quality of slide films varies depending on the brand and type of film.

Modern films, such as Fujichrome, have been designed with reproduction in mind. The film dyes tend to match printing inks better than the older film types. Older Kodachrome emulsions sometimes were difficult to accurately reproduce, despite pleasing colors offered by the film.

A thunderstorm clears over the Union Pacific at Reverse, Idaho, in June 1993. Some magazines run photo features that showcase a single photographer's work. This image appeared in *Pacific RailNews* in an article titled "Etherquest" by Brian Solomon that displayed creative low-light photography as an alternative to more conventional views.

Photo by Brian Solomon
Nikon F3T; 28mm f2.8 AF Nikkor lens; Kodachrome 25

Opposite Page: This stunning sandstorm image was featured in *Desert Railroading*, a gallery compiled and authored by Steve Schmollinger. It was used as the rear cover. J. D. Schmid hadn't intended to make this image, but was set up looking west at Stoval, Arizona, on SP Sunset Route in anticipation of photographing an eastward train in the afternoon glinting sun. A telephoto lens was used to bring in the mountains and crop sky. To the right of the tracks is a dirt road. A succession of vehicles driving down the road kicked up dust which made a spectacular sandstorm image.

Photo by J. D. Schmid
Nikon F3; Kodachrome 25

In June 1961, this photo was virtually unpublishable. Few people would have been impressed by a diesel-hauled Milwaukee Road passenger train in Milwaukee. Thirty-four years later, this view of Milwaukee Road train 101 was seen as a classic image of a bygone era and published in *Rails West* 1995.

Photo by Richard Jay Solomon
Retina IIIC; 90mm Schneider lens; Kodachrome (ASA 10)

David P. Morgan introduced the six-page photo story in 1966 about Southern Railway locomotive 4501 with the headline: "I Could Write a Book." Two years later, the *Trains* editor did just that. He wrote *Locomotive 4501,* published by Kalmbach in 1968. John Gruber made eight photos in the *Trains* story, and most of the photos for the book. Morgan gave him the assignment, in part, because Gruber was available. He took off work with only a week's notice.

Photo by John Gruber

Another factor is the slide exposure. Slightly lighter slides tend to look better in print than traditional "fully saturated" slides. A photograph tends to gain density during printing, so it's better to start with a lighter image. Computer-aided scanning lessens the effects of a dark slide, but it's better to choose a photo that requires less computer work.

Sharpness is another consideration. A soft photo limits the practical size that it can be reproduced. Prepress computers can improve the sharpness, but from an editor's view, it's best to start with a reasonably sharp image. Grain can be a problem. Faster films, those rated at ISO 200 and higher, often are grainy. Grain structure can interfere with the dot patterns in printing, making graininess seem more acute in final reproduction. An editor may limit the size of a grainy photo or, if possible, choose a less grainy image.

Deadlines

Once you've analyzed a magazine's content and style, you can focus your submissions to help the editor illustrate upcoming issues. Avoid missing deadlines, though it's best to submit photos closer to deadlines than months before. Sending photos too early may result in premature return. Or worse, your photos could be "filed for future use" and promptly forgotten. (In the frantic pace of publishing, editors are easily distracted. Photos filed six months ago may be forgotten when photos are selected.)

Magazines are printed a month or two *before* the cover date. An October issue may be printed in August and an issue usually closes several weeks before it is printed. It may be wise to submit those autumn foliage photos in mid-June. If you wait until October, you will miss your window of opportunity.

If a specific subject was just covered in a feature, it probably isn't high on the list of upcoming topics. It may not be featured again for months or years to come.

Finding a magazine's cutoff deadlines is especially useful for submitting news photos. News photo deadlines are later than feature deadlines. Check photo dates published in previous issues.

If an event pictured was photographed on June 10, and appears in the August issue, you can guess the deadline probably is the second or third week of the month. Monthly magazines usually have the same deadlines. Some list publishing deadlines along with contributor guidelines inside the magazine. (These may be published every issue, or once a year.) Others will send you guidelines and deadlines on request.

News photos can be very competitive. If you cover an event, or catch something unusual, act quickly. Process your film promptly, and prepare your slides as soon as they are ready. If you normally send your film away for processing, consider using a local lab that can rapidly process film. Yet, getting your photos to a magazine quickly may make the difference between getting in or being rejected. Getting the

◁

Writing a feature article boosts your chances of getting photos published and helps you develop a working relationship with a magazine's editorial staff. The November 1989 issue of *CTC Board* featured this photo of Conrail's TV-8B at CP 79 east of Palmer on the cover as part of an article on the Boston & Albany. The textured sky left plenty of room for type. The photo was made when the train was stopped on the control siding waiting for a westward Amtrak train to clear the single track.

Photo by Brian Solomon
Leica M2, 35mm f2.0 Summicron lens;
Kodachrome 25 exposed @ 8-f11 f 1/60

Photographer Brian Jennison says. "Prior to my first trip to the CPR in British Columbia and Alberta in February 1982, I read Omer Lavallee's *Van Horne's Road* and studied the maps in Roger Burrow's *Railway Mileposts: British Columbia, Vol. 1.* I noted that as the railroad follows the Kicking Horse River down from Field to Golden, there is a great bend from south to west.

"I reasoned there would be a potentially spectacu-lar shot if I could only get to it. I [pulled] over and scrambled up the side of the hill in knee-deep snow. The sun popped out. Sitting in the snow, I figured the exposure, set my 28mm lens on infini-ty, framed the shot and pressed the shutter. The editors of *CTC Board* cropped it to run on the cover of their February 1990 issue … proving a cover photo doesn't have to be a common 'in your face, telemash nose shot' …"

Photo by Brian Jennison
Nikon F2; 28mm 2.8 Nikkor lens;
Kodachrome 25; f4 1/250

slides on the editor's desk first doesn't guarantee pub-lishing. A good editor should run what he feels is the best photo for the magazine, not what arrived first.

Communicate

Communication can make the difference. If you have a newsworthy image, call the magazine and ask about their deadlines. If an editor needs the photo "ASAP," ask for clarification. If the editor really wants the photo first thing in the morning, ask for a FedEx shipping number. If the magazine pays for shipping, they will be more aware of the photos when they arrive. Be sure the images are something the editor wants.

Calling a magazine editor is one way to find what he or she needs. When you call, it's best to ask for an editor by name, rather than asking for 'the editor.' A magazine's masthead lists editorial staff by name. An editorial staff has numerous responsibili-ties, and the person you ask for may not be available. You may be turned over to a managing editor, associate editor, or a photo editor.

When speaking with anyone on a magazine's staff, state the purpose of your call. Keep your call brief. Editors are busy people and will appreciate your brevity.

If you're trying to make a submission, explain you are a photographer and have images the maga-zine may find desirable. Ask about submission guidelines and deadlines. Briefly describe a specific image you would like to send, but it's often better to allow photographs to speak for themselves.

Ask if they have specific needs, but don't expect an editor to reveal the editorial schedule for the next six months. Unless you know the editor, avoid long-winded explanations of your photographic career or offer critical opinions of the magazine.

Avoid offering information that will cause an editor to draw a negative opinion about you or your images. Describe yourself as a photographer and don't diminish this with unnecessary qualifications.

You are offering material for publication, but no one likes a pushy salesman. Thank the editor for his or her time.

Once you've contacted a magazine editor and submitted photos, there is no harm in calling a few days later to confirm the photos' arrival. Better yet, send an e-mail.

If an editor really likes an image, or a style of images, he or she may offer praise and encourage-ment, but don't expect it. And don't misconstrue a lack of praise as rejection. Contacting an editorial

Brian Jennison has had many photos published prominently on magazine covers, calendars, books, and magazines. His work has been featured at Winterail, and he has authored several books. Brian explains the history of this photo, a cover shot for *Trains Illustrated:*

"The Park series observation car is one of the signature features of VIA Rail's *Canadian* (originally operated by Canadian Pacific), North America's premier scheduled passenger train. This trip to Kicking Horse Pass the week after Christmas 1986 was primarily to capture Canadian Pacific's Rogers Pass helpers one more time before the opening of CP's new MacDonald Tunnel. It would make manned helpers superfluous. I also wanted to photograph VIA's *Canadian* (trains No. 1 and 2), then still operating on its original CPR routing. The station stop at Field allowed time to shoot both ends of the train.

"This picture was chosen as the cover of *Trains Illustrated* for February 1991 for a number of reasons. *TI* was trying concepts that Kalmbach's staid old flagship *Trains* wouldn't consider. Each issue had various themes. The themes for this issue were both 'winter' and 'blue.' There was a 'Farewell to the *Canadian*' article in the issue as well. My picture fit just about every theme the magazine had that month. The art department set the cover up with a 'cut-out' effect and a blue border.

"*TI* was a short-lived Kalmbach experiment. It's unfortunate the magazine didn't last longer, but I've always suspected many of the concepts tested were later applied to a *Trains* redesign that was much improved over the earlier look."

Photo by Brian Jennison
Nikon F2; 28mm f2.8 Nikkor lens;
Kodachrome 25; f4 1/250

office from time-to-time is a good way to develop rapport with an editor. Keep your calls short and specific. Use common sense.

Unless it's requested, avoid calling three times a week. Ask your editor when the best times are to call. Generally, it's best not to call an editorial office first thing Monday morning, on Friday afternoon, or five minutes before the office closes. Mid-morning or mid-afternoon, in the middle of the week, probably are best.

Preparing a Submission

Always treat your photographs in a professional manner. Don't expect editors to respect your photographs if they arrive in a poorly-prepared, unprofessional manner. Too many hopeful photographers fail to properly prepare their submissions. Routinely, editors are faced with snapshots stuffed in letter envelopes, slides wrapped in tissues, and whole collections of random slides that arrived without a proper cover letter.

Each slide should have basic caption information written as neatly as possible.

Or use computer-printed slide labels. Ideally, a slide will feature the location, subject, and date of the photograph. Significant specifics about the image should be briefly noted.

Tim Doherty won third place in the 1999 *Trains* magazine photo contest with this photograph of Conrail's SESA (Selkirk, New York to South Amboy, New Jersey) on the National Docks Branch in Jersey City, New Jersey. Today, this image has special significance because of the background.

Photo by Tim Doherty
Nikon N90S; 180mm f2.8 ED Nikkor lens;
Professional Kodachrome 25 (PKM)
exposed @ f4 1/500

Include your name on the slide, printed exactly as you want to see it published. Print your address on your slides only if you anticipate living at the address for a very long time. It's preferable to include return information in your cover letter and a return envelope. Neatly cross out obsolete address information on the slides.

The reason for this is simple. You never know when your slides actually will be returned and who will return them. Often, an editorial assistant prepares returns. That person will blissfully send the slides to whatever address is printed on them.

Always include a succinct cover letter. Tell the editor what to expect in the package you've sent. Briefly state why you've sent the slides—whether they're for general use, specific submission, news photo, or whatever. If photos are of an unusual event, rare occurrence, or other noteworthy subject, emphasize this to the editor. If you've included a return envelope, indicate this as well. Always ask that your slides be returned when the editor is through with them.

Be sure to include your return address in the letter. Avoid writing criticism of the magazine in your cover letter. Well-meaning criticism is best handled in a separate letter. You may include more detailed captions, however, caption letters often are separated from slides during the editorial process.

It's vital that you put relevant captions on each slide. Include a telephone and/or e-mail address where you can be reached for more detailed captions, should more information be needed.

Slides are best submitted in archival slide-pages. For the best presentation, always use clean pages. Prepare the slides for the worst. Assume the package they are sent in will be dropped, stepped on, and perhaps even run over.

Pack slides between two sheets of stiff cardboard and use a photo mailer (a thick cardboard envelope.) This will protect them from most potential shipping damage. If you are sending via the United States Post

Here is an example of a typical submission letter:

October 15, 2001

Mike Confalone
Railroad Explorer
PO Box 248
Goffstown, NH 03045

Dear Mike:

Enclosed, please find seven 35mm slides and two black and white prints for your consideration in *Railroad Explorer*. You may retain these slides for use in upcoming issues of *Railroad Explorer*. As per your request, I have written short captions to accompany the black and white photographs.

If you have any questions about the photos, please e-mail me at:
Brian@goodread.com

Please return all photographs to me as soon as you are finished with them.

Thank you for considering my work!

Sincerely,

Brian Solomon

Office, use priority mail and get a return receipt or delivery confirmation. Write or stamp on the package: "Photographs, Please do not bend."

How Often to Submit

Consider your first submission a trial run. Few photographers make it big on their first try. Photographers who are published most also are persistent with submissions.

For your first submission, you may wish to send a variety of images that represent the body of

your work. Include different photo styles and angles as well as a variety of subject matter. Be selective and don't overwhelm an editor with a barrage of images.

A single page of 20 well-composed, stylistically varied images should be plenty. If you're sending in news photos, one or two images may be enough. If possible, give your editor a choice of both horizontal and vertical views.

Your first submission may not grab an editor's attention immediately. The editor may review hundreds of slides every week, and perhaps thousands every month. If you are persistent and regularly submit high quality work, it will eventually warrant attention.

Understanding Rejection and Acceptance

If your images are returned unpublished with an impersonal form letter, don't feel bad or be discouraged. Learn from the experience and submit again and again. Just because an editor returns photographs doesn't mean your work is unworthy.

It may mean your photos weren't appropriate for the issue in production. Also, what one magazine rejects, another may accept. A typical railway magazine may only publish between 50 and 100 photos per issue, but may have 5,000 photo selections. That means only one to two photos out of 100 are used.

When your work is accepted and published, consider how your photo is placed in the publication and learn how you might submit more photos that your editor will find useful. Why do you think your editor chose this photo? Was it used full frame or was it cropped? Did the cropping improve the composition? How was the quality of the photo reproduction? Does the photo look good to you in print?

The more you publish, the better you can understand photo selection. If you established rapport with an editor, give him or her a call after your photo is published. Explain that you are trying to understand the editor's publishing needs. And thank him or her for using your work and query about the reasons your photo was selected.

Articles

One of the best way to get your photos in print is by writing articles with them. An author has many advantages over other contributors when it comes to photo submission and selection. The author can submit photos that illustrate elements of the text. Providing a well-written, nicely illustrated article is doing the editor a favor.

Magazines may seek to expand on your illustrations by soliciting additional contributions. This is normal. Remember, an editor's responsibility is to provide readers with the best material. Coming from one source makes it easier, but if additional sources are required, that course must be taken.

Before you spend weeks and months researching and laboring over a 10,000-word, 30-photo, 18-page epic feature, contact your editor and discuss the project. Call to pitch an idea. Discuss the length, breadth, and scope of the piece. If the editor gives you a date, be sure to deliver your work on time.

Being on time is crucial. From an editor's point of view, there are two or more kinds of contributors. One shows a lot of enthusiasm for a project, promises his editor the world, then fails to deliver on time. A rarer kind of contributor listens to an editor's input, agrees to a deadline, then delivers what is promised on time. Being the second kind of contributor will help you get published.

Short articles generally are easier to write and more useful to an editor. Every magazine has limited space and an editor must balance features with news, columns, and advertising. It's easier to place a two-page article than an 18-page epic. If you write an article on a timely, interesting subject that consists of 500 to 1000 words (two to four pages typed) and includes two to four photos, it will be easy for your editor to find space.

Smaller publications often are easier to work with. They need fresh material and new contributors. Larger magazines tend to have a backlog of articles waiting to be published and face tighter editorial space constraints. Work with smaller magazines to learn about writing and illustrating articles.

If you aren't adept at writing, consider working with someone. Perhaps you have a friend who works for a railroad, or know a fellow enthusiast with a story to tell.

Calendars and Books

In addition to magazines, there are many potential outlets for your photography. Each has its own special considerations and it's best to know your market before you submit. Railway magazine publishing probably is the easiest place to start publishing because they tend to use many photographs.

A company that produces railway calendars uses only 12 to 25 photos per calendar per year. Query railway calendar producers for their submission guidelines and deadlines. Often, calendars are produced well in advance so it's especially important to know when to submit. Calendar companies occasionally advertise in railway magazines, especially later in the year.

Carefully observe the types of photos used in previously published calendars. Many calendar producers like to keep seasonal images. If this is the case, you are more likely to have photos selected if your photos clearly depict each season.

If you send 12 clean, high-impact, properly exposed slides of the seasonal themes to a railway calendar company, you have a better chance of selection than if you send a batch of high sun, three-

▶

Opposite Page: Amtrak's *Montrealer* pauses on the New England Central at Palmer, Massachusetts, waiting for clearance to cross Conrail on its northward journey on the morning of Feb. 8, 1995. The New England Central was only a few days old, having just assumed operations from the Central Vermont Railway. At the time, Amtrak was in financial crisis and the *Montrealer* was one of several trains canceled to save money. *Passenger Train Journal* used this image as a news photo in issue 208. It was later published in the *Railroad Explorer.*

Photo by Brian Solomon
Nikon F3T; 35mm PC Nikkor lens; Kodachrome 25 exposed @ f4 for 2 seconds.

quarter shots of freight trains in the summer.

Some railroads publish calendars for their employees. Often, they feature clean views of that railroad's freight trains passing through splendid scenery.

Book publishing is more difficult to break into. It's far more common for book producers (be they an author, publisher, or packager) to solicit photographers to submit work than for photographers to approach them.

One of your best bets for having your photos used in books is to develop a body of high quality published work in railway magazines. If you've demonstrated your ability to supply images, you might find you are asked to submit photos for a book.

Books often are on much longer publishing schedules than magazines. It isn't unusual for a book producer to hold on to slides for a year or more during the course of production. If your photos are selected by a publisher, ask them roughly how long they plan to hold them. This will give you an idea of when you should expect them back.

Publishing arrangements vary widely. In some situations an author is completely in control of illustrations for his text. In other situations, the publisher is in charge of illustrations and the author has very little input. Sometimes book producers will issue lists of their various upcoming titles and photographic needs to regular contributors.

Railroad enthusiast publications are only one potential outlet for publication. This image was only used in a brochure about mass transit. It depicts the Baltimore MTA light rail system against a dramatic backdrop of Baltimore's Skyline.

Photo by Tim Doherty
Nikon N6006; 24-120mm Nikkor zoom lens; Ektachrome 200 exposed @ f6.3 1/500

Colin Garratt: Reflections of a Professional Railway Photographer

"The motivating force of the Industrial Revolution was the steam locomotive. It is a beautiful and sensuous creation—the one living machine.

Also, it is an outstanding subject for photography, arguably Britain's greatest technological gift to mankind.

In 1969, these were some of the reasons that persuaded me to abandon a promising career in marketing to document the world's last steam locomotives, not with record photography but with pictures that expressed their wonder and mystique.

This self-imposed task constituted a unique odyssey. Few people had any faith that I would succeed because I had limited funds, basic photographic equipment and no photographic training.

It was predicted that I would be coming back to the firm within six months, asking for my job. I never looked back. [It was] a non-stop, 100-hour work week for at least the first 15 years.

My income came from publishing and lecturing. My first book was published in 1970, one of the first color railway books to appear on the British market.

The uniqueness of my profession gave me valuable media coverage. That helped the sales of the books and promoted the lectures.

From live presentations, I moved to audio-visual, touring theater shows. These consisted of up to 12 computer-driven projectors beaming multi-vision images onto a panoramic screen, interspersed with music, sound effects and live commentary.

These powerful presentations lasted two hours and contained upwards of 4,000 pictures with as many as 40 projector tray changes. Productions such as "Colin Garratt's World of Steam," "The Great Railway Adventure" and "Rail Romance and Revolution," all based on the global expeditions, played in Britain in the 1980s.

My aim was to spend four months on a world expedition, five months performing the shows and three months writing and compiling books.

The success of the audio-visual shows attracted the attention of British Rail. A working relationship with British Rail led to the formation of Milepost 92 1/2, a multi-media production company and picture library. We are photographers of the railway industry.

Our work for the railway industry mixes in a fascinating way with the historical activities. I run Milepost with a team of five talented individuals. We operate from a three-story Georgian farmhouse in the soft Leicestershire countryside, in the middle of England. We are situated next to the Midland Mainline, 92 1/2 miles north of London.

The company's name and logo are taken from the milepost located immediately alongside the farmhouse.

For the last 12 years I have been a dedicated Canon EOS photographer. The cameras, lenses, and lighting units are breathtakingly good. From the time I turned professional, I have used Agfa Color reversal film exclusively.

Milepost's studios overlook the Victorian Bridge. It was the location where I watched my first trains as a child, more than 50 years ago."

The address for Colin Garratt's Milepost firm is:

Milepost 92 1/2
Newton Harcourt
Leicestershire, LE8-9FH
United Kingdom

Telephone: 0116 259 2068
Fax: 0116 259 3001
www.milepost92-half.co.uk

Colin Garratt flew to Alaska to photograph these three derelict former New York Elevated Railway Forney-type 0-4-4T steam locomotives in June 2000. The locomotives lie abandoned on the Arctic Tundra in Northern Alaska, having gone to work on an ill-starred gold rush railway and laying derelict for upwards of 100 years.

Photo by Colin Garratt courtesy Milepost 92 1/2
Canon EOS 1v; Canon 500mm;
Agfa Professional RSX-reversal 50 ASA

A Burlington Northern freight races through the crossing of Highway 30 at Shiro, Texas, on June 7, 1980. Tom Kline blocked the sun from directly hitting the lens, allowing the train to glint. A wide-angle lens and slow shutter speed accentuates the train's motion.

Photo by Tom Kline
Fujica ST605; Hanimex 28mm lens; Kodachrome 25 exposed @ f8 1/60

North Shore line conductor Gene Bergfeld waits for passengers on the station platform in Milwaukee, Wisconsin. John Gruber stood about 12 feet away, focusing on the conductor's face with a 200mm lens. The electric interurban railroad made its last trips between Chicago and Milwaukee in 1963. Documenting a line's culture is a part of the railroad story. So often, photographers concentrate on the equipment, while Gruber's efforts record the people who worked on the line.

Photo by John Gruber

Opposite Page: Boston & Albany 1409 leads a 47-car freight over the Berkshires near the Twin Ledges west of Middlefield, Massachusetts, on April 13, 1947. Pushing on the back of the train is a 2-8-2 Mikado, No. 1226. This Berkshire-type was built by Lima in 1926, a locomotive named for the hills in western Massachusetts where this type was first tested. A tradition of amateur railway action photography was established in the steam era that typically conveyed the majesty of locomotives at work.

Photo by Robert A. Buck
Kodak folding camera; f3.5 Zeiss Tessar lens

Good railway photographs can be made from many vantage points. This photograph was exposed from the back of a Lehigh Valley passenger train at Lehighton, Pennsylvania, on March 27, 1959. Such a scene could only be made by a railway museum today. The wooden caboose and Baldwin switcher pictured here have long vanished from mainline American railroading. Framing equipment in the passenger car's back vestibule added depth and intrigue to the image while helping to minimize the undesirable effect of a texture-less sky.

Photo by Richard Jay Solomon
Kodak Retina Model IIIC; 50mm Schneider f2 lens; Kodachrome (ASA 10)

Books

Adams, A. *Ansel Adams Photography.* Three books: *The Camera, The Negative, The Print.*
New York: Little, Brown and Co., 1999.

Evans, R. M. *The Perception of Color.* New York: John Wiley and Sons, Inc., 1974.

Feininger, A. *Feininger On Photography.* New York: Crown Publishing Group, 1953.

The Focal Encyclopedia Of Photography. St. Louis: Focal Press, 7th Ed., 1999.

Fujifilm Professional Data Guide. Tacoma, Wash.: Fuji Publishing Group, 2001.

James, T. H. and Mees, C. E. *The Theory Of The Photographic Process.* New York: Macmillan, 1977.

Kieran, M. *Photoshop Color Correction.* Berkeley, Cal.: Peachpit Press, 2003.

Kingslake, R. *Optics In Photography.* Bellingham, Wash.: SPIE Press, 1992.

Kodak Professional Photoguide (Pub. No. R-28). Rochester, N.Y.: Eastman Kodak Co., 5th Ed.,1995.

Krages, B. P. *Legal Handbook for Photographers.* Buffalo, N.Y.: Amherst Media, 2001.

Lynch, D. and Livingston, W. *Color And Light In Nature.* New York: Cambridge Publishing, 2001.

Minnaert, M. G. J. and Seymour, L. *Light And Color In The Outdoors.* New York: Springer-Verlag, 1993.

Neblette, C. B. Photography: *Its Materials And Processes.* New York: Van Nostrand, 1962.

Rowell, Galen A. *Galen Rowell's Vision: The Art of Adventure Photography.* San Francisco: Sierra Club Books, 1995.

Rowell, Galen A. *Galen Rowell's Inner Game of Outdoor Photography.* New York: W.W. Norton and Co., 2001.

Stroebel, L. et al. *Basic Photographic Materials and Processes.* St. Louis: Focal Press, 2nd Ed., 2000.

Stroebel L. *View Camera Technique.* St. Louis: Focal Press, 7th Ed.,1999.

Wilhelm, H. G. and Brower, C. *The Permanence And Care Of Color Photographs.* Vancouver, Wash.: Preservation Publishing, 1993.

Williams, J. B. *Image Clarity: High Resolution Photography.* St. Louis: Focal Press: 1990.

Maps

DeLorme
(produces state atlases and gazetteers for most of the U.S.)
P.O. Box 298
Freeport, ME 04032
Phone: 207-865-4171
Web page: www.delorme.com

Steam Powered Publishing
(publishes regional American railroad atlases)
Dawes Road, Dunkirk, Nr. Faversham, Kent, ME13 9TP, United Kingdom

United States Geological Survey
USGS National Center
12201 Sunrise Valley Drive
Reston, VA 20192
Phone: 1-888-ASK-USGS (1-888-275-8747)
Web page: www.usgs.gov

Ordinance Survey
(British map agency)
Romsey Road, Southhampton, United Kingdom, SO16 4GU
Phone from USA: 011-44 1233 2110
Web page: www.ordsvy.gov.uk/
E-mail: enquiries@ordsvy.gov.uk

Rail Fan Timetables

Altamont Press
P. O. Box 754
Modesto, CA 95353-0754
Phone: 209-577-1307
Web site: www.altamontpress.com

Oxford Junction Press
14 Conlin Rd, Oxford, MA 01540

Weather

Web sites:
www.nws.noaa.gov
www.weatherunderground.com

National Weather Service radio frequencies:
162.400 MHz
162.425 MHz
162.450 MHz
162.475 MHz
162.500 MHz
162.525 MHz
162.550 MHz

✳ Brian Solomon

A second generation railroad photographer, Brian Solomon inherited his passion from his father, Richard Jay Solomon. Brian began railway photography at age 5, when he took a twilight photo of a former New Haven Railroad signal east of the East Haven tunnel, using his father's Leica M3. He earned a Bachelor of Fine Arts degree in photographic illustration from the Rochester Institute of Technology.

After a stint working as a professional photographer, he was hired by Pentrex to help edit *Passenger Train Journal* and *Pacific Rail News*. Later, he was named editor of *PRN*.

A freelance author since 1996, Brian has produced more than 20 books on railways, including the 2002 title *Railway Masterpieces*. He has published more than 2000 photographs in many calendars, brochures, and publications including *Railway Age*, *TRAINS Magazine*, and the *Journal of the Irish Railway Record Society*.

He has traveled widely, visiting railway operations in more than 20 countries around the world.

✳ John Gruber

Railroad historian and photographer John Gruber is president of the Center for Railroad Photography and Art (www.railphoto-art.org) and editor of its journal, *Railroad Heritage*. He is coordinating the Center's project, "Representations of Railroad Work, Past and Present," funded by the North American Railway Foundation. A free-lance railroad photographer since 1960, he received a railroad history award from the Railway & Locomotive Historical Society in 1994 for lifetime achievement.

Gruber is contributing editor to *Classic Trains*, preservation columnist for *Trains*, and co-author of *Caboose* (2001) and *Travel by Train, the American Railroad Poster* (2002). He edited *Vintage Rails* magazine from 1995 to 1999. Gruber has a bachelor's degree in journalism from the University of Wisconsin and has done graduate work in the historic preservation program of the UW's department of landscape architecture. Gruber and his wife, Bonnie, live in Madison, Wisconsin.